YOU CAN DO IT!

Ignore what they tell you! Use Your "Unfortunate" life circumstances to your advantage! Do not ever let anyone tell you, you can not do something! Always tell yourself You Can!

JAMES CUNNINGHAM III

© Copyright 2024 by James Cunningham III

All rights reserved. No portion of this book may be reproduced, stored in a retrieval system, or transmitted in any form or by any means—electronic, mechanical, photocopy, recording, scanning, or other—except for brief quotations in critical reviews or articles, without the prior written permission of the publisher.

ISBN:

eBook ISBN:

Unless otherwise noted, Scripture quotations are taken from the King James Version. Public domain.

Strong's Concordance. Public Domain.

Cover design by Rica Cabrex

Printed in the United States of America

TABLE OF CONTENTS

Introduction	7
1. Play The Cards You're Dealt!	9
2. Can I?	17
3. "Take Care Of The Big Things First"	25
4. Life Is A Game Of Inches	35
5. Find The Fuel That Lights Your Fire	43
6. I Have Good News And Bad News	49
7. Closed Mouth Don't Get Fed	57
8. I Should Just Jump Out Of The Window	69
9. Could Of, Should Of, Would Of	77
10. It's Not What You Know, It's Who You Know	85
11. What's The Difference Between Them And You?	97
12. Use The Towel Or Throw It In, Your Choice	107
13. Living In 4D	113
14. How Much Do You Have In Your Cup?	121
15. It's An Inside Job	131
16. Love	139
17. What Do You Want Your Dash To Represent?	147
Conclusion	155
Bibliography	157
Acknowledgments	159
About the Author	169

This book is dedicated to everyone who aspires to live their purpose in this thing we call life and to remind you DO NOT ever let anyone tell you, you cannot do something but more importantly always tell yourself YOU CAN! I wrote this book with the intent to bring hope to at least one child growing up in the circumstances like I did and to be a light to all. Thank you to all the teachers from Walton elementary and Thomas Jefferson Middle School that told me I would never amount to anything. How I would be lucky if I could make it to see eighteen and not in jail or dead. This book is for everyone from all walks of life especially those growing up in the worse conditions of every city across the world here is some HOPE for you. To the individuals who are abused, counted out, misunderstood, overlooked, underprivileged, I put my story on paper to prove to you that YOU CAN DO IT. Wherever you are in life I want you to keep going.

INTRODUCTION

YOU CAN DO IT! This phrase has led to many inspired individuals around the world and offered people an immense amount of *hope*. Deep down, HOPE is something that we all need and desire. Without it we become sick, but when we have it, it is like a tree of life. The impact of having hope is immeasurable, and the same can be said for not having it. I have come to learn that "which *hope we have as an anchor of the soul*, both sure and stedfast, and which entereth into that within the veil" Hebrews 6:19.

We all have learned at some point about the purpose of an anchor to keep a ship safe and secure at a desired location or to help control the ship during bad weather. However, to accomplish these vital purposes, simply having an anchor is not enough. The anchor must be solid, dependable, and used properly at the right time and place. Regardless of the size of your anchor, it is imperative to understand its attachment to your soul. Allow me to use my personal journey to show you how you can overcome the challenges and obstacles often referred to as "bad things." We all will have bad things happen in our lives, but the mindset we have toward these experiences will make or break you. The degree of which our hope is built upon will determine if we can use it when necessary. It is up to you to use it at the right place and time on your journey.

The information within this book is my personal note of encouragement. It will show you how to be resilient and overcome hard things. My story will help solve the problem of wasting time for the ordinary individual looking to better navigate life at the expense of time invested and hardships. My mother always told me that if someone else can do it, then so can you. I hope the information written will give you the courage to believe this for yourself. I want to thank you in advance for reading my story and giving me an opportunity to allow me to share parts of my journey to give you some hope. I look forward to taking this journey with you and pray you use my experience to your advantage.

Chapter One
PLAY THE CARDS YOU'RE DEALT!

"Hey, Jimmy, why do you have that up on your wall?" Dot asked. "Because I want to, and it's none of your business. Get out of my room and go do something!" I shouted back at her. I remember having this conversation with my oldest sister growing up in public housing provided by Cuyahoga Metropolitan Housing Authority, known as the projects on West 25th in Cleveland, Ohio. This part of Cleveland was unique as we had a melting pot of all races, and anything you could imagine seeing happened in my hood. We did not have the big home and fancy things, but we had all the necessities, including three sides of tough love from one value-driven hard-working woman, who I like to call my rock. Whenever I look back, I can say I truly enjoyed my childhood. But like many around at the time, I had mixed emotions about the cards I was dealt. Before we talk about some of the cards, I want to give a special shout-out to my siblings for helping make my upbringing exciting and always keeping me on my toes.

Me with my sisters, Dot and Milly

Now let me get back to what my sister was referring to. It was a certificate I had received from my grade school teacher for outstanding work. It was something I was so proud of, so I decided to hang it up. It was the first time in my life I was proud of something. I did not have much to hang up in my room, but of the few things I did have, this would stare at me every day. Have you ever received a certificate for outstanding work of some sort? How long did you keep it? Did you hang it up? For me, this was the first certificate I ever received, and something told me to hang it up. So, I listened to "the voice" in my head. The quote at the bottom of that hard-earned certificate is the main reason for getting so much attention

> *"A journey of a thousand miles begins with a single step."*
>
> — LAO TZU

Attributed to Chinese philosopher Lao Tzu, the quote above encapsulates all aspects of life. It highlights the importance of taking things one day at a time when any journey, professional or personal, seems too tedious and daunting. Yes, you have probably seen or read this quote before, but I had the privilege of reading it over three thousand times in my room during my childhood. I know it is not a trophy or expensive wall art, but as a young boy the quote on this piece of paper gave me hope. It reminded me about the importance of persevering and so many other things. I did not know at the time I would need this embedded into my brain as events would start to unfold, which would test my fortitude.

When you are barely at the age of accountability and you start to experience life-altering trauma, quotes like this will help carry you through. I have learned that most people have or will endure some type of trauma in life. I am sure there is another young boy or girl going through the same exact things I endured. So let me share a few of my rough days to help you get through yours.

I remember it like it was yesterday. It was after school over at a relative's house where we would often stay until my mother was done working at the beauty salon. This day, though, I was tired after school, which is not typical for an eight-year-old boy. I was invited to nap with my female relative who was twice my age. Not long into the nap, I felt something touching me. It was not appropriate, and the next thing I know I was told to get on top of her. Scared and confused, I did as I was told. The emotions running through my little body were nothing I had experienced before. But thanks to her mother coming home unexpectedly, I was pushed off her and told to "be quiet" and "I better not say anything." Her mother did not think anything of it, and eventually I was able to pull my pants up before being picked up to go home.

This same type of incident would occur at a later date with another family member who used to "watch me." This time it was by an individual whom I happened to be their favorite. She even treated me like a son of her own in some ways. I have since forgiven and even prayed for these individuals, as no child should ever experience this type of abuse. It did not seem like anything was wrong at the time, but as I grew into a young man, I came to realize that before the age of eighteen at least 16 percent of boys and 25 percent of girls will experience this same type of abusive behavior [1].

To the parents reading this, I encourage you to pay close attention to the individuals you allow to be around your children. Protect your kids at all costs! It is also worth noting that even when you strive to protect them, bad things can still happen. In this case, I want to encourage you to not place blame on yourself. This is a difficult thing to stomach as it happens every day right under some parent's noses. As you can imagine, these experiences led to a complete lack of understanding on what sex was all about. That following summer, I would involuntarily learn more about what it meant as I was introduced to gang life and running the streets with my big brother, who happened to be my cousin. He was the first male I wanted to grow up and be like. He taught me the ways of Vice Lord, including the handshake, and would take me with him on all types of adventures with the gang.

I was the little "safe" that police officers would not think about searching if they would attempt to arrest us. To this day, I am not sure whose idea it was to put a pistol and crack in my possession. But whoever it was sure was clever. I do, however, remember one adventure where we would sneak out the house while my aunt was sleep. It was a chilly night at approximately 11:00 p.m. We climbed through the window on our walk, which seemed like a marathon to some young harlot house. I am pretty sure he would have left me back home if he would have trusted I would not tell on him.

When we arrived at the destination, I thought there would be a reward waiting for me, but it did not take long to learn that my prize would be a front-row seat to the action under the bed. As I hid under the bed, I heard the sounds of love-making and the odd conversation taking place—along with the parents of this girl coming home unexpectedly. All of a sudden, we were now both hiding under the bed. I am glad we made it out because who knows what would have happened. Those adventures were cool at the time, and I eventually started to look forward to them. That was until he decided to go on an adventure without me with the expectation that I would be the one who would let him in when he got back home. But he would find out I was in a deep sleep and blew his cover. My aunt eventually found out he was sneaking out of the house, and he was not happy with me.

It would not be many adventures to look forward to following this occasion because my big brother was taken from me shortly after these antics to serve a lengthy jail sentence for committing armed robbery. I cried like a baby the day I found out he was sentenced. I felt lost and did not know what I would do with myself. I wondered who would teach me how to become a man. He was the only one I viewed as someone to look up to. If I learned anything during the trips we took, he taught me about the importance of family sticking together.

My cousin paid his dues and served his time. He went on to earn a degree while incarcerated and has since come home and put together the things in his life that matter the most. Despite the cards that are stacked against him, he is doing well in all areas of his life. He has avoided being incarcerated again, and this is something we all must respect about someone who has made a few mistakes in life. He might not know this, but this is something I would put in the bank of things I am proud of about him. We do not talk as much as when I was a young boy, but whenever we have words, I can say he always has positive things to say and is constantly thinking about doing positive things.

Once he got locked up, I was happy to find out that our new next-door neighbors had boys around my age. First thought that came to my mind was that maybe I could find a friend who could fill that void. It sure was not happening at home. I would find out sooner rather than later there was going to be some inconsistency at home in the male role model department. I love my mother with all my heart, but her selection of men was very odd to me growing up. First of all, none of the men resembled each other in looks. They all had different career paths, core values, and religious beliefs. One was Muslim, another was a Jehovah's witness, and the others did not care much about religion. As you can image, it was hard for me to not question religion and why things were so inconsistent. I saw firsthand as a young boy what my life could amount to as a man if I wanted to use drugs, physically abuse women (I tried to stab one of them who had my mother pinned down), smoke marijuana, and drink Budweiser beer every day, or simply stay home and bet on horse races while reminiscing on what my life could have been.

Nothing against any of these individuals, as I have a special place for them all in my heart. Despite their struggles, I was able to learn a few things from them all. I do have to say my mother tried very hard to give me a father figure four times, but I still had that void of having a traditional father-son relationship. None of these men would teach me the biblical understanding of manhood or what matters most in life. There was no training a child up the right way so I would not depart. Each of them had difficulty correcting me, so this contributed to a void in respect toward men in authority. I am thankful to have crossed paths with men later on in life who would teach me these very important things I lacked, whom I mention in the chapters to come.

I knew my cards were different, but I as time went on, I always thought about that quote: "*A thousand miles . . .*" I made sure to lean on it. I have never been a big fan of playing a game of cards, but I am a big fan of playing the cards of life. I have learned in life you cannot change your hand, but you can play what you have been dealt to the best of your ability and avoid trying to play the hand you wish you were dealt. Wherever you are right now more than likely is not where you will finish, especially if you commit to making sure that is not the case. Maybe it was not a quote for you, but I challenge you to look at the events of your life and the small yet often overlooked things that carted you through. I bet you can find something, or at the very least a moment when you listened to the voice also.

Challenge #1 Stop what you are doing and reflect on these set of questions: How have you played the cards you have been dealt? If it were possible, would you trade your cards in for another hand? If you answered yes to trading in your hand, I encourage you to take more time to reflect and realize you were dealt a great hand also. The key is how you play the hand you have been dealt. I hope you are ready for the ride I am about to take you on. I recommend you grab some popcorn, pour your favorite glass of wine, light that cigar, or whatever it is you like to do in your leisure. Everyone we meet has a story to tell and lesson to teach if we have the openness to hear it. *I would love to hear how you have played your cards. If you are willing to share, please use the hashtag #YCDI so we can collectively bring light into the world. Your story deserves to be heard too.*

Chapter Two
CAN I?

Can I help you with your bags? Can I cut your grass? Can I have your cans? Can I have your program? At first glance, it might sound like a few questions that a professional scrounge would ask. These are all quite different and questions I would ask strangers in my youth, which will stay with me forever. Do you remember any specific questions from your youth that resonate with the person you are today? I am sure if you have never thought about it, you could find at least one. Let me tell you about these and what they did for me.

These were all questions that would lead to getting some chips (not the ones you eat, which, by the way, are my weakness) as we called it, or as you may refer to it nowadays as "earning a dollar." Like many kids today being raised in unfortunate environments, I did not have the privilege to go to my mother whenever I wanted something. I am actually very thankful for it being this way as I look back. I can only imagine how hard it is when you grow up privileged and never have to work hard. Growing up we called these types of individuals "spoon fed," which is a label no one respects.

At the time, though, I had a different idea of what things should be like when it comes to having money. I learned very early from my rock that "money don't grow on trees" as she did not have "a pot to piss in," and "closed mouths don't get fed." These ended up becoming famous sayings that I heard not only in my home but throughout my hood quite often. When I look back, they were some of the best sayings I could have heard. Being given these metaphors, or what some may refer to as hood proverbs, became valuable life lessons.

As you can imagine, I would need to become thoughtful and resourceful to get the things I wanted. Although I had everything I needed, I can assure you—like every little boy—I had plenty of things I wanted to possess. For me, it started with collecting sports cards. In the early 1990s, this habit kept me out of trouble. I would become obsessed with finding ways to improve my collection. Whether it was playing one-on-one basketball, gambling, rolling dice, or any other way to make money, I found ways to get more cards. Speaking of trouble, if I went looking for it, it was right outside in my backyard. My mother taught us not to ever go looking for it, which I tried to avoid it at all costs. Although when mom was not around, it was much harder to stay on the right path.

Most days I would leave my house in the mornings after she would head off to her hair salon, but before this, I would also hear the followings words like clockwork: "Get y'all ass up!

Ain't nobody sleeping in around here." She would follow it with, "You snooze, you lose." I think what she was really trying to tell us were a few proverbs from King Solomon, but in her own unique way, lol. I guess that was better than the traditional alarm clock everyone and their mother once had. (Mom, when you read this, I would like to emphasize that it says in Proverbs 27:14 you should not wake your neighbor with a loud voice in the morning, and you for sure ignored this in our household, but I still love you.)

This beautiful, hardworking woman was our personal alarm clock. She operated in such a style similar to a correctional officer and had justifiable reasons as to why. Although she had no baton, and we were not behind bars, she would bang on our bedroom doors each and every day like clockwork. We had no luxury of being sluggards sleeping in all day. I give credit to her for not only forcing us to get up when we did not want to, but more than anything she was the example of grinding. I learned very early that being lazy was not going to cut it in her household.

My mother taught me if you want something you have to get up and go get it. She sure did get up every day, and I am sure most days she did not want to but made it happen anyway. Most days she worked twelve-plus hour days at the salon, so that meant we had to do some things on our own. All we had to do was play our part and "hold things down" while she was at work. Making meals for ourselves was one of them, as well as doing our chores and homework.

The lesson of accountability here would help me later in life, although most days we wished she were home. My sisters and I would get creative when we got in the kitchen. I still think I had the coldest sandwich in the house as I used to whip up a mean bologna sandwich. I preferred mine extra crispy on the edges with a few slices across the middle. I would fry the bread in the pan and throw some cheese and mayonnaise with mustard on that bad boy, then pour myself a glass of Kool-Aid. This was my version of a five-course dinner.

In life, we all have things we should be thankful for, and the welfare assistance we had at the time which allowed for us to eat is something I do not take for granted. I am not ashamed to say we grew up on food stamps and government assistance, and that help is something I am thankful for. My mother "did what she had to do" just like every single woman on welfare. I remember it like it was yesterday, riding my bike like a true cyclist to the corner store with those food stamps to play her numbers and pick up my goodies. Those were the days of complete innocence as I had no idea of the financial situation we were in. I even wore our status as a badge of honor when standing in the line to check out at the local bodega.

However, it did not take long to realize that I could not pay for my haircut with food stamps. Yes, I once tried to pay for my haircut in food stamps. After coming to the realization that my barber only accepted cash, this is where I had to sweet talk my mother into earning allowance. When the negotiation was done, the allowance my mother afforded me still would not be enough. I was given my portion of chores in the home and, if done consistently as instructed without having to be told to do so, that would earn me ten dollars every two weeks. At this time, it was enough for a seven-dollar haircut at the local barber, whose name was Martin. This old man gave the best fades and lineups around town. I would get up out of that chair feeling like the hottest thing since slice bread, followed by the occasional KFC three-piece meal I enjoyed once I got home. But I got tired of having no money after the weeks of chores.

One day, a conversation with my neighbors sparked an idea that was genius at the time and would trump allowance. We discussed a way we could all make some additional money. It was time to get creative as we previously had gone through all the various different lengths to get a few bucks we knew of from collecting aluminum cans to trying to cut grass with a manual mower. My friends and I decided it would be best if we worked a full day shift carrying bags at the local grocery stores. Each person coming out those doors would be greeted by some young boys with their courteous words: "Excuse me, sir or ma'am, can we help you carry your bags?" I am still in awe of the outcome. Not only did we make more money, but we also learned how to overcome speaking to strangers in the process. I am thankful the grocery store did not run us off, which they easily could have. I believe it was because we were respectful of their customers, and we looked presentable.

We decided we should have our own uniform of wearing a plain white T-shirt (Mike, when you read this, I still remember you tried to one-up us with your V-neck!) and khakis. We worked as many days as we could all to earn some money so we could get a pack of cards that we would eventually try to flip for more money. I wanted more than to just flip a pack of cards.

I was looking for ways to get an edge myself, so on most weeknights I would gladly tag along with my parents as they exercised their gambling habit at the racetrack where they bet on horses. While they were busy trying to "hit their numbers," I was busy collecting programs.

One day I had an idea that would guarantee me revenue while at the track, so I decided to ask a stranger if I could have his program as he exited the place. I would watch the gamblers exit after losing their money and throw the program away, which had no more use for them. I thought new customers could use that same program at a resale value, and I was proven right. My discount was better than the front office, and they all gladly purchased from me with no hesitation. I will never forget the day I sold twenty programs and generated twenty dollars to go purchase some popular flip-flops. I eventually upgraded the flip.

Right to left me, Moe, Mike, Marty (bottom)

It was a normal fall afternoon after school, and I ran into a friend who pulled out a wad of money; nowadays it is referred to as a stack. This was not a normal scenario of seeing someone with that much money. I asked Shorty, "Where did you get that money from?" And his response was, "I have a trick." I told him, "Well, show me the trick." And that is all it took for me to be introduced to learning how to become a ghetto pharmacist without the drug store. Later that week I got my allowance, and he promised me that if I gave him ten dollars, I could double it really quick. He did not lie! It took less than five minutes to exchange ten dollars and turn it into twenty. What I did not know at the time was that I had just got my first "dub," and boy was I excited when I exchanged that small stone for twenty dollars to my first client, whose name was Ray. Not once did I think of the ramifications in the event. I was caught in the act of doing this. All I had on my mind was that I'd just found an easy way to double my money. It was nice for a change to have some money left over after getting a haircut and buying KFC. I gave Shorty another ten dollars to flip, and just like that I was another innocent young kid dealing crack in the local neighborhood.

Did you know the chances of someone between the ages fourteen and nineteen distributing illegal drugs in poverty-stricken neighborhoods are one-fourth? [2] I did not know this at the time, but I fell in that number, and many are still falling prey every day. If you are of this age and have been offered to sell drugs, I want to encourage you to learn from me. Tell them thanks, but you have a better idea of how to make money. I promise you there are more legal options to make more money than distributing illegal drugs, and I am willing to bet you that I have a few ideas that you have not been introduced to. I am more than willing to help point you in the right direction. I would love to hear from you, and if you are willing to share your story, please reach out to me so we can point you in the right direction. Your life has meaning, and everyone has a purpose. I hope to help you find it! Speaking of finding, let us talk about a couple of people who found me and helped forever change the course of my life.

Challenge #2 I want you to think about the questions from your youth that resonate with the person you are today and write them down. Record how you feel. I challenge you to share this with someone close to you. *I would love to hear about those questions. If you are willing to share, please use the hashtag: #YCDI.*

Chapter Three
"TAKE CARE OF THE BIG THINGS FIRST"

Have you ever had a meeting with complete strangers, and the outcome ended up being divine? I did not realize the magnitude of a meeting I would have at fourteen years old, but decades later I am fully aware it was divine. Like I challenged you in the previous chapter to think back throughout your life, I really want you to do so here as well. We all have strange encounters in life. And believe it or not, like it says in Hebrews 13:2, we have also entertained angels unaware.

1998 sure was an interesting year for me. It was my freshman year of high school, and if I had to pick one year that would always stand out, this one is at the top of the list. This was the year I had a revelation of something different planned for my life. Although I had this revelation during a time one should not be proud. I was high as a kite sitting at my next-door neighbor's house, and I had an experience that confirmed my belief in the power of the one who revealed his name to Moses in Exodus

3:14 as I AM, AHAYAH in Hebrew (see *Strong's Concordance*, H1961) that no one could tell me otherwise. It started with the thought that I had about our similarity to ants. I randomly stated to everyone, "Hey y'all, have you ever thought we are just like ants? Just like when we step on an ant and kill it, the same thing can happen to us if a meteor landed on us right now." As you can imagine, everyone wanted me to shut up, but I continued as the high was really kicking in. I was sitting at the table in the living room, looking at the tub of Vaseline, and said, "Have you ever thought about who created Vaseline?" At this point they all laughed out loud and said, "Man, would you shut up? You are blowing my high." Well, I did not shut up. I continued and attempted to lead a discussion about creation. I said, "If there was no such thing as life, what would everything be?" This did not warrant a response as they were all busy watching Martin laughing and trying to tune me out. I continued and said, "There is a creator for everything. Someone took the time to make this table, just like someone took the time to shoot us out. We know who we come from and give credit to our Father, but if we keep going back, we can trace who created who but have to stop once we get to God. The crazy thing is that no one can take the credit for creating the Creator of all things."

Once this happened, I felt compelled to share this testimony with others. I had to get it off my chest, but most of my friends thought I was ridiculous and just laughed at me whenever I revealed things to them. I did not feel so bad once I read that "Our Saviour" or Yashaya in Hebrew (*Strong's Concordance*, H3467) was also thought crazy by his friends and family. This was during a time when I started to notice my passion of sharing deep things was increasing. It is also ironic that the verse in Exodus is 14, and at this exact age I would experience a few other things that now make sense on what was to come. I would also like you to know this was also around the same time my mother, for the first time, tried handing me a King James Bible to read, and I had no interest in it whatsoever. I opened it to Genesis, then closed that thing so fast and decided to hit the streets as it seemed more fruitful. I could not understand how people could read the Bible. I tried reading the first verse in Genesis, and it was ridiculous to me. Chances are it was due to the brain cells I was frying as I experimented more and started to cave to temptation.

Reading was not on the priority list, but getting some money definitely was. My mother did not know at the time how I would go about getting it. Well, I at least thought she did not know, but come to find out she had an idea. I thought I could get away with my actions, but little did I know there were eyes watching my every move not only on the streets but from above. The day I had undercover police officers hem me up, they completely searched every one of my pockets besides the one where I had an eight-ball of crack. I will never forget the state of mind in that very moment of thinking my life was over. I still remember that feeling of being so scared as they searched my pockets. There was a deep combination of fear and sadness going through my mind that day. I tried to convince them they had the wrong person as I attempted to use my T-shirt to prove it. That day I wore my high school football shirt and tried to make them see I was a "good one" because I was a Saint Edward student. Luckily, they did not go all the way down my front right pocket, which is where the drugs were located. They let me go, and I rode my bike home thinking, *How did this just happen?* I sure dodged one that day, but I also knew it was my first strike.

The next strike was when I was robbed at gunpoint with a double barrel shotgun put to my head at the same age. This was at the same time people were getting robbed and killed for Jordan sneakers and leather bomber Avirex jackets throughout the inner city. I felt like I was protected that night and spared, but I knew it was also strike two. That night I had a sit-down with my mother and stepdad, and I realized that God was telling me, "I am giving you one last chance to turn your life around." I knew something had to change, so that night I decided to never sell drugs again! It was very tempting as it took time for clients to get the message to stop contacting me on my beeper when they got no response. Not to mention I still associated with all the individuals who were distributing in my neighborhood.

I see this thing we call life as one beautiful journey, filled with encounters throughout the different chapters or phases of our life, along with the puzzle pieces we need to all find before time runs out. At the age of fourteen, my book could have ended. Time could have run out for me. I am thankful to have been spared. When you are looking at a double barrel shotgun smack-dead in your eyeballs, it will not take long to have such thoughts. That night, while walking down W.31st on the way to my girlfriend's house, is a night I will never forget. On our twenty-minute walk, Mike and I attempted to take a shortcut.

What I learned that night is that *if you try to take shortcuts in life, you will come up short*. It was God's will that I was spared as the circumstances could have been completely different. It is worth noting that many people I ran the streets with did not have the same outcome of protection. I could have served a lengthy time in jail, been murdered, or even placed on death row. All these things happened to individuals I ran around with in the streets. The icing on the cake for me this year was when a random woman on the Greater Cleveland Regional Transit Authority (RTA) bus told me, "God wants you to know he has something special planned for you, and it is a calling on your life." She turned around, did not say another word, and then proceeded to get off at next the stop. It was at this very moment I knew I had to stay on the right path. To this day, this is one of the most interesting interactions I have had with someone unintentionally. Some might say she was just another drug addict who seldom rode the RTA, but I am positive she was an angel.

Here is where the Director of Redeemer Iglesias Crisis Center comes into the picture to help me stay on that path. This beautiful soul has served her community for most of her life. Diane was the one in the neighborhood everyone felt comfortable with, and she knew that we were selling drugs but never told on us. She thought I was doing it to afford my schooling. This was not the case, but nevertheless she was approached by a retired couple that same year who wanted to "sponsor" a kid, and unknowingly she suggested me. Who knows how my life would have turned out if she would have suggested someone else. I asked her why she chose me over anyone else, and she said, "I know you could go on and do great things." When I heard these words, it gave me hope.

This suggestion led to a very important life-changing meeting with my mother, Fred, and Sheila Kressierer. They came into my life at the right time. I did not know it, but my mother was just about to pull me out of school as she could not afford the tuition. I would have transferred back into Cleveland inner city schools and gone down the same path and had strike three quickly. When we met with them, it was a meeting that I felt was an agreement, which was bigger than people meeting in a room to discuss helping my mother pay for tuition. They agreed to help pay for my tuition, but I had to maintain at least a 3.0 grade point average. Also, when I got older, I had to promise to give back by doing the same thing. This agreement was sealed with a handshake. That day I had a boost of hope and vowed not to let anyone down.

It was during the meeting I would learn a valuable lesson about life. In front of me was an empty stemless wine glass along with sand, various rocks, and water. The experiment started with Fred pouring the small rocks into the glass, followed by the big rocks in which it could not fit. He then took the rocks out and put the big ones in first, followed by the small rocks, and looked at me with the most serious look on his face. He let me ponder his words, then followed up with, "Jimmy, take care of the big things first, then the little things in life will be easy."

Fred would explain that the big things represented the most important things you need to get done in life, and school was one of the big things. He further explained what the small things entailed. This was my first lesson on prioritizing my life. I can credit Fred with being the first man to teach me on this subject. Prior to this meeting, I did not care for school as much, but that would soon change as I now had my ticket out the hood.

Rock experiment kept as souvenir

This sure was an interesting time for me, and it is hard to believe this all happened within the same calendar year. I took the rocks home with me and have kept them as a prized possession. They now sit in a place where I can see them daily to never forget about the meeting. Over the years, they have been a constant reminder of not only my promise to Fred but also to always keep my priorities in order. How ironic is it that selling rocks would be my downfall, and now I get to look at the rock experiment every day to never forget that lesson.

Mom and me having dinner with Fred and Sheila

Challenge #3 I am sure you have had time to think about your life and reflect on the encounters you have had with "strangers" who have come into your life. Whether good or bad, I want to assure you that despite all the bad things we have in the world, there are also a lot of good people. The individuals I mentioned in this chapter are all good people that I am blessed to have crossed paths with who provided hope and helped me take care of the big things. It all started with an inch of love from my neighbor. *I want to challenge you to also be on the lookout to help others gain inches.* I am confident you can have a positive impact on someone, just as Fred and Sheila had on my life. Speaking of inches, flip the page and let us talk about the significance inches have on life.

Chapter Four
LIFE IS A GAME OF INCHES

I once read a true story about the best man to ever walk earth, and he literally went an entire forty days without food and water. Can you imagine the agony he went through? Have you ever attempted something like this? If so, I would love to hear the outcome as I am sure something miraculous must have taken place. The longest I have ever lasted going without food or water was twenty-four hours as I usually fast each year in September during the day of atonement by abstaining from water and food with the sole objective to afflict my soul. The first time I did it, I promise you I barely made it a full day. Yes, this is nothing in comparison to forty days. I cannot only imagine having forty times the pain, and I am very confident I would need some extra ministering like this individual had to have. I am sure over time many individuals have attempted to see how long they can fast, and many outcomes have been documented. There was a study done on the topic of fasting, which concluded that a person can only survive eight to twenty-one days without food and water [3]. So one must wonder how this individual could go forty days (Luke 4:2) without food and water, not to mention he overcame a lot of temptation the entire time.

It has been said that we can go four minutes without air but only four seconds without hope. Why? Because hope provides the power that energizes those without life. I believe all we need is hope and our desire to succeed in life will awaken. Once hope is activated by faith, it does not matter about the circumstances. I have learned it is very hard to stop the individual with hope, but for the individual without it, the battle in life is almost over. We have all learned that life is not fair. This concept is deeply rooted in the true battles we all face. I love the reminder in the book of Ephesians 6:12: "For we wrestle not against flesh and blood, but against principalities, against powers, against the rulers of the darkness of this world, against spiritual wickedness in high places." This is the true battle, and once we accept the fact that life is going to punch us in the face, we should start preparing for it. It will then become a mindset and give us a change of perspective.

I view this four-letter word HOPE as important as H_2O. I see the *H* as Hope. The Merriam-Webster definition states that hope is "a desire accompanied by expectation of or belief in fulfillment." In the Bible, the first time hope is mentioned is in Ruth 1:12. The meaning of the word *hope* (*Strong's* H8615) is an attachment to the thing that we long for. It reads in Hebrews 11:1: "Faith is the substance of things hoped for, the evidence of things not seen." In the previous chapter, I shared with you a few individuals who brought hope to me at a paramount time in my life. I am firmly convinced that without the hope I was provided, I would have had more of the wrong thoughts about life. Fun fact: the word *hope* is mentioned at least 174 times in the Bible. Regardless of what you believe, it will give you basic instructions before leaving earth. My favorite verse on the subject of hope reads in Romans 15:4: "For whatsoever things were written aforetime were written for our learning, that we through patience and comfort of the scriptures might have hope." One might ask why is hope mentioned so many times? I do not know the answer to that, but what I do know is that throughout my life I have most certainly had to look for it.

Let me share a few moments when I was seeking hope. The day in elementary when Mrs. Jones told me I would not live to see eighteen years old. I was looking for hope, and hoped that she would be around long enough to witness how I would be used by God for his glory. The day I had a double barrel shotgun to my forehead I was looking for it, hoping that the trigger wouldn't move one inch. The day undercover police searched me, I was looking for it, hoping they would not look one more inch as it would have been a different outcome for me. The day I was in the middle of a fight that led to a shootout at the skating rink, I was looking for hope. Had I stepped out into the crowd one more inch, maybe it would have been me that was shot. The day I let my father wear my ring, which would eventually be pawned for drug money, I was looking for it as I was hoping to see it again. Unfortunately, that never happened, and the outcome would lead to major trust issues. A lesson learned here is that if you do not forgive someone, you will carry that baggage around for years, and what is within that baggage is their darkness. It took me twenty-one years to release this baggage and forgive him. If you struggle with forgiveness, I want you to know it does not mean you have to accept the behavior of the individual. It means you choose to forgive so you can let go and move on with life. Mark 6:26 says, "But if ye do not forgive, neither will your Father which is in heaven forgive your trespasses." At some point, we all need to be forgiven. Okay, so back to more times when I was searching for hope...

After graduating college, I rigorously trained for one year before participating in professional football combines where I drove from Ohio to Indiana, Florida, and New Orleans, all in hopes of becoming an NFL player. When I took my state exam to become a licensed insurance professional, I was looking for it. And when I heard the words "you pass," I knew hope was real. I can go on and on, but by now I am sure you get the point. The inches of hope we need can be found everywhere around us. We often miss them, and sometimes we do not fight for them. Let this be a reminder to you that they all add up over time and make all the difference in the world. The worst part is that we lose our edge when we stop fighting for it, and we need that edge. It is what keeps us sharp enough to make big plays when the opportunities arise.

I learned through football and track the impact one inch can have on your outcome. It could be the difference between winning and losing the game or race. Whether or not you have participated in a sport and regardless of your skill level, you can learn the same. The point here is that in life there will be a series of opportunities, and often the difference between how things will turn out is just one inch of hope. It is our individual duty to make decisions to put our hope in the right things no matter what cards we have been dealt. In the process, I believe it is healthy to never forget about the people, places, or things that have brought you hope throughout your life. Whenever I have the chance to visit my hometown, I make an effort to stop through and reminisce, and to never forget where I come from. The way I do this is to sit in the same place when I was a little boy where I would think of ways to get out my environment. This is the same location where undercover police had me hemmed up. Many were not fortunate enough to make it out of my environment, and this I do not take for granted. So regardless of what I have going on or the weather condition when I do visit, I will always roll through the hood. Things might not look the same, but the reminder will always be there.

Sitting on the stoop of Redeemer Crisis Center

I have been asked many times what I hope to accomplish with this book, and the answer is simple: *I wish to bring hope to at least one person*. Hopefully, that will be you or the next reader. What I can guarantee you is that if you keep reading, you will be able to apply some things within this book that will help you in your life. Hopefully, you will gain an inch.

Challenge #4 I challenge you to never stop fighting for the "inches" in your life. I also want you to take a moment before the next chapter and reflect on the times in your life you were looking for hope. *I would love to hear about it. If you are willing to share, please use the hashtag #YCDI.*

Chapter Five
FIND THE FUEL THAT LIGHTS YOUR FIRE

If you look up the definition and history of the *N* word, what do you see? When you think of this word, how does it make you feel? However, you feel about the word, I believe some words can propel you in life if you allow it, and that is what it did for me. It was in a school setting I would learn the magnitude of this word. First let me give you some perspective about my high school. I was only one of the four minorities who graduated in my senior class of 181 students, and we were all members of the varsity football team. A majority of the minorities were from the inner city, such as myself. Several of us would commute to school every day using the RTA, which for me took several buses to reach my final destination. From age fourteen to eighteen, I would get up between 5:30 and 6:00 a.m. most days to get ready in time and walk in pitch-dark to catch three buses to school. The highlight of my day usually happened in the cafeteria. I would forget about the commute as I always looked forward to when I had money to get warm cookies and milk or the occasional biscuit and gravy. When I really had it going on, I could get something from Tina's before school.

The 2001 Varsity Football Team: (first row) T. Smith, J.Scherach, N. Bryce, J. Kilbane, L. Rios, G. Luczyk, M. Staron, B. Middaugh, P. Stack; (second row) M. Czajkowski, E. Claxon, W. Norman, J. Cunningham, R. Stover, J. Hines, F. Valentine, J. Haney, R. Keenan; (third row) J. McManamon, J. Miller, D. Pride, J. Sabogal, B. Pierce, K. Quinn, J. Sikora, C. McGuirk, D. Miranda, D. Hawk; (fourth row) J. Giachetti, J. Reese, K. Horton, J. Lesco, C. Dills, D. Kelly, T. Dorsey, B. Ready, C. Sroka, C. Rose, S. Carney; (fifth row) J. Berry - trainer, M. Belko, F. Costanzo, C. Rawlings, D. Surtz, J. Foster, J. Boone, E. Smith, E. Zaletel, K Bringman; (sixth row) Coaches D. Holian, S. O'Donnell, M. Levindofske, Head Coach J. Gibbons, Coaches M. Schmittel, D. Waitkus, B. Walnsch, S. Niedzwiecki (seventh row) Coaches D. Scanlon, J. Whaley, Steve Hart - Trainer, Coaches D. Gdovin, M. Angelo, M. Corte

On a cold afternoon during the winter of my sophomore year at Saint Edward High School located in Lakewood, Ohio, it was in the cafeteria where this word would truly serve its purpose in my life. At this time, I did not understand the power of a single word and how it would help shape the course of the next decade of my life. As I was enjoying lunch on a not-so-normal day with a special guest visitor having lunch with us at "our table," I tried to put my best foot forward because I might just get noticed myself. That day the head men's basketball coach for University of North Carolina was in town to recruit a future player who would go on to help him win the NCAA National men's basketball championship in 2005, and boy was it a day.

The typical lunchroom conversations amongst a bunch of ego-driven, testosterone-filled competitive young men is one memory that will always stay with me of my high school experience. The conversation this day would eventually make its way to me and another individual, who would eventually go on to win the 2006 Heisman Trophy as well as help lead the Ohio State Buckeyes to a National Championship in 2002 along with getting drafted to the NFL.

I can remember it like it was yesterday, hearing the statement, "Nigga, you ain't shit and you will never be shit." This was followed by a few individuals laughing after the statement was made in front of the now-retired University of North Carolina head coach. On any normal day, I would not have thought much of the word because I grew up using it part of my regular daily vocabulary amongst my childhood friends. But that day, I was embarrassed yet fired up to prove something from that day forward. As you can imagine, we had a verbal fight that eventually got broken up by a few students and faculty. I went home that day with a fuel lit in me that had been waiting to be ignited. Just like a car, it is almost impossible to run without some type of fuel. Wherever you are driving your car (aka self), I believe it is a great idea to choose the right fuel. Some fuel can be bad for your engine. This fuel for me, on the other hand, was top-notch premium.

I repeated that statement over and over in my head that night and so many times over the years. If you had real estate in my brain that day, you might have suggested me checking in to seek mental help. I say this with all due respect to anyone who might be struggling with any mental conditions, because I know my mental health was unstable during this time. In my mind I had no outlet, and I did not have the courage to speak with someone about the event trauma. I recommend if you are experiencing any sort of trauma to seek help, or you can take the approach I did, which would allow me to eventually experience something inside of me that I did not know existed.

The ultimate life lesson I learned is that through every situation we encounter, we can look for the good in it if we seek it. The beautiful thing about this for me is that I would find the single fuel that would light my fire. This one single life-changing moment pushed me at practice, in the weight room, on the field, on the track, in the classroom, and eventually in the boardroom. I had to prove to myself that I am worthy and would amount to something. I give credit to this individual for making that statement as I am not sure if I would have had that fuel inside of me ignited. I firmly believe we all have had or will have moments in our life where we can use a circumstance or situation to our advantage, and I share this moment of mine to inspire you to find yours.

At any time if you want to be fueled up, I have a simple exercise for you. Grab a piece of paper and pen, then write down the most painful comments ever made to you by people that you loved: former colleagues, coaches, bosses etc. For example, on my paper it would read, *This person said*, "You will never be shit." *Another person said*, "You will never amount to anything." You write these types of things down and then you read it. See how you feel after you read it, and go there when no one else is around. This will produce emotion you can use anytime at your leisure. If for whatever reason you do not feel comfortable following this exercise, I recommend you find a way to use the negative things people have said to you as fuel. I sure did use this and will continue to do so as I encounter all negativity in the future.

I hope if you are seeking to find your fuel that you find it and use it to your advantage. Some refer to it as reaching in the "cookie jar," and it is a metaphor coined by Goggins from his book *Can't Hurt Me*: "The **cookie jar** is a place in my mind where I put all things bad and good that shaped me. Some people try to forget the bad in their life. I use my bad for strength when needed, great lessons learned. In that **cookie jar**, I pull out whatever I need for the task at hand."

Okay, so back to looking up the definition. I did some digging on the word, and I found out that the word was used going all the way back to biblical times. Let us go to history school and discuss something they did not teach us about the original spelling of the word, which was Niger. Eventually another *g* was added on to degrade the one *g*. When the word is used today, it is meant for degrading, but the word itself is not a degradation. In fact, the original people who were referred to as the word were teachers and prophets in Acts 13:1. The first disciples were referred to this in Antioch. After learning this, it gave me an entirely new perspective. These men endured such labels, and yet they remain focused on the task at hand. So my hope is that you take this experience and apply it to your life in some way to help propel you.

Challenge #5 Write down the names of all the individuals who have said the most painful comments ever made to or about you. Next, write down what was said. Finally, record how it made you feel. This, my friend, is what you call *free fuel*, and anytime you need to get gassed up to do something, I want you refer to it! *I would love to hear about those comments. If you are willing to share, please use the hashtag #YCDI.*

Chapter Six

I HAVE GOOD NEWS AND BAD NEWS

Have you ever been dealt "bad news"? I am not talking about the type of news we hear or see on TV or social media every day that is dictated by the media to control your thoughts. I am talking about hearing something from someone you have never met, not expecting the words they share with you to be life-altering.

My senior year in high school was the first time I was given the good news/bad news talk. It was the first week of my final season and an ordinary day at football practice. I played wide receiver, and as we are doing our position drills out of nowhere, I fell down and could not move my legs. I was carried off the field, and my mother arrived in time to rush me to the hospital. I knew something was injured, but I did not realize how severe things were. It turns out I injured my back very badly. As we drove to the hospital, the only thing I thought about was when I could get back on the field. They did several

X-rays, and I thought that would be the extent of tests needed, but boy was I mistaken.

Once we finally met with the doctor, which seemed like forever, he came in the room and told me he would have to check my spinal cord by completing a rectal exam. I still have a tough time thinking about that moment. Just the idea of anything going inside me makes me cringe. I didn't realize it at the moment, but this would be the first and only time I would ever agree to be violated. He ended up doing a system of tests used to define and describe the extent and severity of my spinal cord injury to determine future rehabilitation and recovery needs. This is something that is ideally completed within seventy-two hours after the initial injury.

Once done with the test, he said with a tone of zero care, "Well, I have some good news and bad news. Which one do you prefer to hear first?" I decided to hear the bad news first. He informed me that I would never be able to play competitive sports again. The good news was that I would be able to recover from the injury and walk again. His final diagnosis was that I slipped two discs, bruised my spinal cord, pulled several muscles, and pinched a few nerves all in one singular motion at practice. Mind you, this injury involved no physical contact, so initially it was hard to believe what I was hearing.

To say it was the worst pain I have had to physically endure up to this point in life would be an understatement, and my back has never been the same since then. I became very depressed while listening to the doctor say, "You would never be able to play sports competitively for the duration of your life. But the good thing is that you will recover and be able to walk again." You might be wondering why would someone become depressed from hearing this news? Well, because in my mind sports was my "ticket" out. Every child growing up in the ghettos across the world trying to "get it out the mud" can relate to this because everyone is looking for a ticket out, and I thought I had found mine. That day in the hospital I cried like a baby in front of my mother as we looked at the X-ray, but I still had this thought in the back of my mind: *Do not believe what this man is saying. He is not God, and I refuse to allow this man to determine my fate.* It was at this very moment where I would learn a valuable lesson. This moment allowed me to know that the Most High whispers to us in our pleasure but screams at us in our pain. It is like a warning sign for us and should be used to motivate, guide, and gauge things.

I was determined to prove the doctor wrong and get back to competing and finishing out my senior year. As I started the rehabilitation process, I could not stand in a straight posture or walk without some type of assistance for two months. This was a humbling time, and I truly appreciated just having the ability to walk from that point on. I would also go on to miss out on the majority of my senior season, not to mention I was bedridden a majority of this time and could not attend school. They had me on a very high dosage of Vicodin, Percocet, and muscle relaxers to ease the pain. Several nights I would go to sleep and wake up forgetting I had the injury, almost falling out of the bed as I woke up. I am surprised I did not become addicted to pain pills like many other athletes I know. At this point, I decided that regardless of the cards I was dealt, I was committed to doing the rehab necessary so I could come back and finish things out and hopefully get to the next level. There was not a plan B option anywhere in sight. I had to finish what I'd started. Although most would have given up playing football, I decided not to listen to the doctor. I would persevere by doing whatever it took to get back to normality.

Throughout the majority of my athletic journey, I did not have the pleasure of having my parents attend every game in the stands, cheering and rooting for me. My mother was busy working and could not take time off. I admit it hurt watching all my friends have their parents present at events, but I have to give my mother credit as she did a great job lifting me up emotionally during my recovery period. During this time, she was the main one who encouraged me and told me to have faith. She never let me think it was over. She would remind me in her own special way by saying, "It ain't over until the fat lady sings." Turns out she was right as she has been about almost everything pertaining to my life. I was eventually able to come back and was cleared to play again just before our rival game. I wanted nothing more than to be in the game and help my team win. We had an undefeated season, and it was a miracle I was able to make a comeback within the season. Eventually, I would go on to continue my athletic career at the University of Mount Union where I was a member of the football and track and field team. Unfortunately, I reaggravated my back during my sophomore season of track. It was during my NCAA provisional qualifying 55-meter run where I slammed awkwardly into the wall at the end of the run. Unlike the beautiful indoor track facility you see today on campus, we did not have an appropriate runway at the time. They made things work by placing a high jump mat against the wall to absorb the shock as we ran into it. If you have ever watched a vehicle crash test simulation, this is exactly what we looked like when we made impact.

I eventually did not run at NCAA indoor championship as I had intended to that season, but I did become friends with pain all over again. This time, though, I had the foresight to know that the pain would visit me again and the visualization to see myself overcoming that pain before the encounter. I was fortunate enough to tap into the emotional state of the previous victory of rehab when needed to remind myself of what I was capable of overcoming. The following year as a junior I qualified to run at the NCAA outdoor championship, but my coach opted not to let me run. I am still not happy about that decision. I feel we were robbed of an opportunity and believe we could have at least earned All-American status.

I did not dwell on this, and when it came time to run the following season, I made sure he could not hold us back. When senior year came, I was able to qualify in multiple events at NCAA outdoor championship and bring home a national championship title with my 400-meter relay team. The best part of this accomplishment was proving my coach wrong and looking him straight in the face when he handed us the trophy and saying, "I thought we wouldn't win," followed by having him get in the pic with us. At this time of my maturation process, I truly thought that my head Track & Field coach, John Homon (USTFCCCA Hall of Fame), did not think we could win as he told me straight up to my face the week leading up to this meet that we would not win. Now I can appreciate the push he gave us as he knew how to push our buttons. He knew I was more motivated by someone telling me that I could not do something more than positive affirmations. In the following picture, if you look closely at my face, I have this look of *I told you we would win,* but this was more for the third-place team who talked trash about us online that season and at the meet before the final race. There were some unhappy campers to the right of me, and they were all mad when we took the title.

Left: The day I reaggravated my back | Right: Nic, Johnny, Pierre, and me

We still hold the school record as well as several stadium records from that year. I still physically suffer from back pain to this day but would not have it any other way because I learned some valuable lessons along the way. The pain we all go through in life is meant to build us up stronger and help us become the best version of ourselves. Here is a change in perspective on the subject. I would be willing to bet that everyone you respect went through some kind of pain you do not know about. They all got through it, and if you ask them about the pain they have had to endure, you will be surprised at what you will find out.

I have a few questions for you about pain:

- What do you do with your pain?
- Do you let it break you or redefine you?
- Are you able to outlast your pain?
- Are you going to get a reward for your pain?
- Will you make pain your fuel?
- Are you ready to meet pain when it comes knocking on your door?

Whatever you decide to do with your pain, I bet you can use it for your advantage, whether you believe it or not. In the book *Awaken the Giant Within*, Tony Robbins goes over the pain pleasure principle: "Everything we do we do for a reason and it's a driving force behind all human behavior in life is out of our need to avoid pain or desire to gain pleasure." I encourage you to keep a healthy perspective on pain as you experience it in your life. Use my story as a reminder to never stop believing, even when others who are designated as the professional and are supposed to know best discourage you. Pain is inevitable in this life, but misery is optional. In the Bible pain is mentioned over fifty times, and in Revelation 21:4 it reads, "And God shall wipe away all tears from their eyes; and there shall be no more death, neither sorrow, nor crying, neither shall there be any more pain: for the former things are passed away." This is the only time there will be no pain! So it is best to do the work required while we still have a heartbeat and fight through pain. Do not be soft; have faith. It can be the difference between giving up on your dreams or not. You must go in the direction of your pain to find your purpose. I want to give a special thanks to my favorite chiropractor Dr. Jordan Burns, who has helped me improve the health of my back. I am more aligned than I have ever been as a result of working with him over the years. I would like to suggest reading his work if you want to learn about holistic health hacks, mind medicine, or how to supercharge your sleep.

Challenge #6 I challenge you for the duration of your life for every negative situation you encounter to look for the positive from it. This exercise will help foster a more optimistic and resilient mindset, as well as encourage creative problem solving. *Okay, so tell me . . . Have you ever been delivered bad news? Did you turn it into something positive? I would love to hear about it. If you are willing to share, please use the hashtag #YCDI.*

Chapter Seven
CLOSED MOUTH DON'T GET FED

You are probably wondering who said this famous saying. Well, the first time I heard it was out of my dear mother's mouth. Another one of her fine proverbs that will stay with me forever. If you look this saying up in the urban dictionary, it will tell you it is a saying popular among adults, which means, "if you do not open your mouth, you will not get what it is you want." I wonder where she got this saying from and who coined it; they must have had some wisdom.

The first time this saying hit me was in a huddle on the field of Kent State University. This moment was my last high school football game played, and we were on the brink of being eliminated from the OHSAA Division 1 football playoffs. Our goal of being state champions was ripped away. My team was ranked as one of the top teams in the state. Coming into this game we were 11-0 going against another top contender, who was 10-1 in the state. We had the higher ranking in the state going into the game, along with projections to win. This matchup featured several individuals who would go on to play at the next level, including the winner of game would determine the most likely winner of Mr. Ohio between the top two running backs in the state. No, I was not the running back; I played wideout.

This season we broke several school records (most wins: ten, most points scored: 437, least passes intercepted: 2, all which still stand). We were ranked top in northeast Ohio, so it is safe to say we were very confident we could and would win this game. Little did we know, on the other side of the field was a team who was out to send us home crying. Boy did we cry as we left that field. The final score was 26-42; Eagles were taken down by Raiders. I do not regret many things in life, but looking back I wish I would have listened to my mother sooner as I can recall several times in this game when this saying was whispered to me.

The first time that voice whispered to me was when I finally spoke up in the huddle after a time-out and told my offensive coordinator Scott Niedzwiecki, "He cannot cover me, Coach. I am open. Please throw me the ball." Next play it was thrown my way, but just a few feet overthrew in front of me or else I would have taken it to the house. No knock on my quarterback as I was fortunate to have some of the best throw to me. This one would eventually go on to be a star quarterback for the Air Force, and the other went to Ohio State and became a Heisman Trophy winner. Although the pass was not completed, what I learned in that moment was the lesson my mother had been trying to teach me the entire time leading up to this point. The only problem was it was almost too late in this game.

I have since learned it is never too late in life, only when your heart stops beating. I have had many moments in my life where I chose to not listen to the advice, and after that huddle each time that voice whispers to set me straight. In my business endeavors, the first time I encountered the voice was during a conversation with the president of the company I served for fourteen-plus years. I was able to build a unique relationship with him. I first shook his hand at my first attended annual company convention. This is where the top-ten percent of the company, usually one thousand plus qualifiers, would assemble at an exotic location and partake in a three-day recognition party. The impression I would leave on him in Puerto Rico would lead to another choice encounter a year later. I would be asked to look out for someone close to him, and by doing so credibility was earned.

By me saying yes, it would validate more about myself and help jumpstart our relationship. This would eventually lead to obtaining his direct contact info, with the "if I ever needed anything" conversation to follow. It turns out I did need something, and it was to hear from his mouth and gain some clarity on advancement opportunities, along with consideration of a promotion with my career. I wanted a bigger piece of the pie and was willing to make the crust from scratch. I just needed confirmation that it was a possibility.

The day I called to ask him a question about the possibilities for promotion would lead to a phone call I will never forget. It was the same day LeBron James announced he was taking his talents to South beach Miami to play for the Heat organization. Being from northeast Ohio, I witnessed firsthand the many heart-breaking emotions throughout the city as his announcement was being made. That day I would arrive home to tears throughout the entire neighborhood. I told my wife it was time to call "The Man" (as I had his name stored in my phone) and ask some questions. It did not take more than a week after this call where eventually I would have to inform my family and friends privately that I would be taking my talents to Indianapolis, Indiana. This would turn out to be one of the best decisions I would ever make. Well, at least I thought I was the one directing my own steps at the time. Later I would learn (after reading Psalm 37:23) it was never me.

This was one of the most exciting and scariest times of my life. I had just been pushed into a promotion with my company that required my family and me to leave everything behind to go start a new life and business from scratch in a city we did not know anything about. I am thankful for my close friend and business partner at the time (Jamison Weatherspoon) who was not only along for the ride but helped push the needle. We were in our mid-twenties and ambitiously looking to take over our territory and that we eventually did with the help of so many. It would be remiss if I fail to mention how IP Harris and John Ophals helped lay the foundation. We quickly made a name for ourselves, won international awards, and accomplished a lot in the four years together enough for us both to earn our degree from the University of Adversity and go on to successfully run our own agencies independently. I learned a lot about the process of starting a business from scratch, along with how to successfully operate a multimillion-dollar organization and ultimately what it took to sustain it while having growth.

Pictured left to right: Marcus Smith, Me, Roger Smith, Jim Surace and Jamison

In this endeavor, I was selected to serve consecutive years on the company executive council and was the youngest minority to ever do so in the history of the company. I was blessed to recruit, train, develop, and lead several championships teams and serve so many people in the process. My goal was always to leave people better off after having met me. One thing I know for sure is that there is not one single person who is worse off after working with me. But yet countless individuals who were able to change not only their life but generations to come. We gave back with time as well as resources in the community, broke a lot of records, and built a championship culture that would eventually be voted Forbes "Happiest Companies to Work" and recognized as one of the Best Places to Work in Indiana and Top Workplace in Indianapolis. From my amazing assistant Emily to the thousands of entry level representatives who were contracted on including the fifty plus thousand customers this vehicle opened the door for so many individuals who would eventually become the best version of themselves while achieving financial prosperity. The fourteen-plus years of dedication to this cause and over thirty million in quality work allowed me sell my business and retire at a very young ripe age of thirty-seven and pursue my passion. Something I am forever grateful to have been able to accomplish several years ahead of schedule.

When I started my career in financial services, I was just barely over the legal age of drinking, and I kept the PHD (poor, hungry, and driven) given to me from my upbringing very close to me. I came into an industry that I did not know much about. I had to overcome a lot in the beginning, starting with proving my mother wrong. She was the first person to tell me I was stupid for pursuing a career that had nothing to do with the degree of which I obtained. As a parent, I can understand her thinking and desire to protect me from wasting my education. The way she initially felt about this career move was not positive. I got the message loud and clear when I attempted to complete a mock presentation with her. At the end of the presentation, she gave me some raw feedback. She took a deep breath and asked me if I want to know how she really felt and proceed to say, "Jimmy, if you think people are going to listen to you and take you seriously, you must be out of your rabbit ass mind. I can't believe you went to school to get your degree and are going to let it go to waste." My initial thought was, *Okay, you might have a valid point.* But I knew something about this career opportunity that she had no understanding about and that it was very lucrative. I made it a goal to prove her wrong and one day get her to tell me that she was proud of me. The positive that came from her feedback was that my presentation truly was not good enough. This advice was the reason I went back to the lab and did the work required to ensure it was good enough so that when I went live with real customers, they would listen to me.

Looking back, this was some of the best advice I could have ever received as I would go on to be the top producer in the organization my first month. There were hundreds of representatives throughout the organization in Ohio and plenty who had years of experience on me, but I would beat them all. The mentality I had was "make it happen or watch it happen to someone else." I learned through my athletic endeavors how hard work could beat talent when talent does not work hard enough. Not to mention when you have talent and willing to be one of the hardest workers in the room good things will always happen. I had no problem working half days (twelve-plus hours) seven days per week to make things happen. I made at least five hundred-plus calls and completed over fifty door knocks each week working in lower-income neighborhoods. Had several doors slammed in my face, called derogatory names, and overcame objections like it was riding a bike. Which, by the way, here is a pro tip for anyone in the financial services world looking to achieve greatness: embrace the word *no* more than hearing yes. You will be told no a lot more than yes. And if you embrace this ahead of time, the likelihood of you taking things personal is slim.

This is one of the many things that defeat people who come into the industry, let alone the work required. I will never forget the days of racking up miles, driving around Ohio, treading through snow one appointment after another as it helped mold me into a true grinder. I did so much grinding, the miles I accumulated were so high, and the overage cost was more than the value of my vehicle when I turned it in. That would be the last vehicle I would ever lease as I learned my lesson not to lease vehicles when you drive for a living. I loved the performance-based opportunity with the ability to control my own income. I knew that by doing these things, the reality was that in fifteen-plus years the only individuals who would know I worked late would be my daughter and wife. This is why it was imperative to get out of the rat race and build a business. The landscape has since changed to a virtual world in this industry, but everyone who came up in this era are what I like to call the true dogs.

Although my mother had reservations, she would be the first person to help me secure meetings with prospective clients during my training period. Her assistance helped me gain confidence in what was possible. When I made my first sale before completion of Steve Surace training class, I knew I could go on to make millions with this vehicle. I also saw firsthand how this could come to fruition through the servant leadership from Jim Surace and Marcus Smith. They taught me about the law of compensation through valuable lessons on serving people and the rewards that come with it. Each day I was reminded that my income was commensurate with how many people I served and how well I served them. I got to determine my level of compensation because there were no limitations on how many people I could serve. One of the most important things I witnessed working with Surace-Smith was that it was possible to do business with integrity and never compromise your values. Seeing this gave me hope and guidance on how I preferred to operate my businesses. I want to encourage you that you can do the same in your endeavors. Yes, having the right vehicle matters, coupled with good leadership and mentors who make a difference, but it is no excuse not to serve people and do it with integrity. As long as you are coachable and willing to do the work, I believe everyone can be successful because everyone can look for ways to serve others. I have to caution you not to let pursuing worldly success (read Mark 8:36) be the thing that defines you as I was also taught a valuable lesson on this early on. There was a saying from one of my mentors that helped put things in perspective on success and has stuck with me.

> *"It's not about how many millions you can make. It's about how many millionaires you can create."*
>
> — SIMON ARIAS

This saying changed my perspective early on about the importance of serving people. He is one of the most decorated individuals to grace the financial service industry. I was so fortunate to have the ability to learn from him early in my career. Our relationship started with a question after a workshop about the difference between various levels throughout the company. His mentorship played a huge role in my success, and this saying was one of the many things in my career that I would go on to use as a measuring stick for a job well done. Now I would never take credit for any individual success. But the numbers do not lie, and I would need more than two hands to count the number of individuals who have made over a million in earnings that once worked within my organization, and plenty more to come who I put on who are well on their way. I can say none of this would have ever been possible had I not opened my mouth at the end of that workshop.

Let us now discuss how opening your mouth applies to personal relationships. I have learned that we all leave relationships for various reasons, but more times than not it is because we feel we are not getting the love we need or deserve. Unfortunately, we blame the other party when our desires are not met. Yet the reality is, chances are we have not asked for what we want or need. The one thing often forgotten about is that there will always be negotiations in the process. Regardless of the outcome, I believe it is imperative to bring something of value into the equation in which we all have been blessed with the ability to do. I want you to think about how often you express to your partner exactly what you want or why you want it? When was the last time you shared with your partner how you feel when you get the thing(s) you need? Well, how can you expect to get what you want if you do not ask for it? How can you even expect to receive the things you say you want if you are not physically, mentally, emotionally, or spiritually present within the relationship to receive them?

Now, there are times when you must remove yourself from a relationship. However, this is not what I am talking about. I am talking about when you remove yourself by taking your mind, your body, your heart, and your soul out of where you are being loved because you are not getting what you have not asked for. Removing yourself in that way is not only self-destructive, but you can ensure you will never get the very thing you say you want. Is it because you may not believe you deserve those things you long to ask for? I want you to know you are worthy. Do you know there is a relationship out there where you will never be let down? There is someone who will sacrifice it all just for you. I hope you find this relationship. What I learned from the saying is that you must always speak up. Most will tell you only when the time is right, but my question for those individuals is: "When is the right time?" I encourage you to not suppress what you have inside and let it out. It could be the difference between having the ball in your hands or never seeing it.

Challenge #7 I challenge you to embrace any time you can speak up for yourself and practice being assertive. *I would love to hear about your moments of opening your mouth. If you are willing to share, please use the hashtag #YCDI.*

Chapter Eight
I SHOULD JUST JUMP OUT OF THE WINDOW

Growing up in the projects, we became hood acrobatics with some of our antics. On any given day you could find someone doing competitive handstands, backflips, or cartwheels. Now I never got backflips down, but there was a stunt I was happy to accomplish. Let me tell you about this stunt my friends and I used to pull off. One day my next-door neighbor was in the process of getting a good ole fashion butt-whooping by his mother, and I heard every minute of that encounter as we had very thin walls that connected our dwelling space. I just happened to be in my room playing Sega Genesis after making a quick run to the corner store.

Picture this: I was in the middle of stuffing my face with my favorite bag of chips at the time, which were Flamin Hot Cheetos (those things were crack in a bag). As soon as I tipped the bag back to enjoy those last crumbles, I heard a window bust. This was no ordinary window bust sound; it happened to be someone that jumped out to escape. He landed on the roof of the shed, and next thing I heard was, "Don't worry. You have to come home" from his mother. That whooping must have been top-notch to jump out the window. On any given day you could hear someone throughout the neighborhood getting "lit up," as the parents would call it, and most days I was able to successfully avoid it. I must admit I received my fair share growing up, and they were definitely lit, but this day I had no clue why he was getting lit up and what would make him jump out a second-story window. This was the first time I ever thought about what it would be like to jump out a window. These thoughts would all be involuntarily. The next time I thought about this act it would be voluntarily, and the outcome was not to land safely.

The day I had voluntary thoughts of jumping out of a window was after a long day of school and practice. It was toward the end of my senior year. I suppressed a lot of negative emotions and thoughts during this time of my life. This is where I started to think all the years of getting up at 5:30 a.m. walking in pitch dark to catch a three buses to school from Cleveland to Lakewood was a waste of time and the years of sacrifice were pointless. Each day I got closer to graduating, I came to the realization time was ticking down to be awarded an athletic scholarship. For most student athletes, their careers end naturally when they graduate from high school because less than 7 percent of all athletes advance to a career at the NCAA level [4]. My dream was to get an athletic scholarship and go on to play football at the D1 NCAA level. Regardless of being a "late bloomer" and not starting to play the game of football until my sophomore year, I was hopeful and confident I possessed enough skill to go on to the next level. Now having not played 80 percent the majority of senior year due to injury, I also had enough common sense to know my senior season would ultimately be inadequate according to Division 1 recruiting standards. But again, that hope was still present. It says in Hebrews 6:11 to "hope unto the end." I began to hope, and during this time it started to become the anchor of my soul. We all have the choice to choose our anchor in life; this happened to be mine.

Things became real for me the afternoon in the library of my high school on the special day for senior athletes who signed their National Letter of Intent (NLI). For those who do not know about this moment, it is a very unique day for all athletes. National signing day is the culmination of a long recruiting journey and a moment where you realize all your discipline, sacrifice, hard work, and dedication has paid off. The National Letter of Intent (NLI) is a legal contract between prospective athletes and NCAA institutions.

The contract states that the athletes agree to attend an NCAA institution for one academic year and that the NCAA institutions agree to provide athletic financial aid for one academic year. I had the luxury of watching my good friends make their commitment to their respective schools while their families attended the celebration. In the background is where you would find me clapping, cheering, and smiling for them all as they individually signed and put on those hats. But while I remained undecided deep down, I had reached the point of depression, or what some would call mental instability.

At the time, I did not realize the severity of dealing with this, but I have come to learn each year there will be several athletes that will go through this same experience. The American College of Sports Medicine (ACSM) did a study and the data indicated that approximately 35 percent of elite athletes suffer from depression [5]. Approximately one-in-five adults live with a mental health condition during their lifetime. While physical activity is excellent for brain health, sports participation is not entirely protective against mental health challenges. On the surface, many athletes appear "okay," but usually what is going on with their inside will be revealed.

It was in a car ride home by "G" where how I was feeling inside would be revealed. I would make a comment to him that did not stay in the car as I hoped. This man was the parent of a fellow teammate who lived nearby, and he would often look out for some of the inner-city kids like we were his very own. Some of my teammates and I called him a booster. Most boosters get a bad rap, but this man really did things for me and others out of love. He was someone who did live up to the royal law and love his neighbor. I witnessed firsthand what it is like to do something for someone who cannot pay you back. For example, he was kind enough to give me twenty dollars once for food. Little did he know that money came in handy. Had he not given me money that day, I do not know if I would have been able to catch the bus to and from school that week, or possibly get food. "G" listened to me and did not judge me as I told him, "I should just jump out the window. What is the point of living anyways?"

The way he responded to me included wisdom and clarity. Although the book of wisdom (Proverbs) states you should seek counsel, that day it was not my intention and yet I received it. This comment I made to him would also make it back to my coaches and principal. That very next day at school, I was immediately met by Scott Niedzwiecki, my assistant coach who was the best offensive coordinator I ever played for, and we had an intimate walk around the track that morning. He listened more than speaking, yet he spoke life into me. It states in Proverbs 1:5: "A wise man will hear, and increase learning; and a man of understanding shall attain unto wise counsels." I am thankful to have had a coach at a time in my life that was able to give me wise counsel. I believe most football coaches out there are only concerned with the "W" on the scoreboard, but he defined what coaching is all about to me. He confirmed that it will always be bigger than wins and losses and more about making a difference in an athlete's life, regardless of their skill or background. He revealed to me the art of walking and talking with people and how it is a great way to connect. I believe in this principle and have found myself doing the same for others throughout my endeavors. To every athlete reading this, if you have a former coach you can still call, text, direct message, Snap, Facebook, FaceTime, then you had a coach who put you first and created a lifelong caring relationship with players. I promise you this is not the majority, so consider yourself lucky and cherish those relationships. I have been very fortunate to play and run for all respective hall of fame coaches from my high school to college athletic journey. What they all have in common is the lasting impact they were able to have on each athlete and their ability to help us become better individuals. Reminder to the coaches reading this book: When you care about the person more than the player who wears the uniform, you are more likely to earn their trust, respect, and loyalty. They will run through a brick wall for you and smile while doing it. When it is over, the impact you make will be over a lifetime, not just a short season.

Pictured: John Gibbons (OHSFCA inductee 2015) addressing team my junior year

Here are eight things players want in a coach: one who cares, one who makes it fun, one who is honest, one who is competitive, one who is not afraid to challenge, one who builds relationships, one who is passionate, and one who can teach. Coach Niedzwiecki possessed all these qualities and proved to me that one coach believing in you and investing in you can change the trajectory of your entire life. The lesson I learned from this incident is that our greatest threat will always be on the inside. He helped me defeat that internal battle just by listening and, in the process, I learned it will always be you versus you. The harder you are on yourself the easier life will be on you. The road to achieving your goals and becoming the best version of yourself will not be an easy road to take. No matter the road you must take to get there, it is always better than being a copied version of someone else. On that road you must stay strong through it all. You can be physically strong but mentally weak if you do not master the battle in your mind. What is inside of you must be stronger than what is on the outside. Do not let the adversary diminish what was put inside of you. Keep your candle lit and search the inward parts. Go inside to know yourself so you can defeat yourself.

In the book *13 Things Mentally Strong People Don't Do*, Amy Morin wrote a beautiful breakdown on the subject, and I would highly recommend reading this book to keep a good perspective on being mentally strong. If you struggle with this part of your life, I would recommend you schedule time each day and take care of your spirit, mind, and body. Each day we all have an opportunity to grow stronger in these areas. There are so many ways to feed yourself with the proper amounts to ensure growth and avoid neglection of these things. Regardless of how you choose to stay strong, the point is to never stop doing it. To the individuals out there who are on a lifetime journey of winning the battle in your mind, I encourage you to keep trusting the process.

Challenge #8 I challenge you to learn from your setbacks and never let a day go by without doing something to get stronger mentally. *Have you ever thought of jumping out the window? I would love to hear about it. If you are willing to share, please use the hashtag #YCDI.*

Chapter Nine
COULD OF, SHOULD OF, WOULD OF

If I had money deposited into my bank account for each time I heard one of these statements growing up, I would for sure have more currency. In most environments, I overheard these types of conversations, but it would be in my house where this topic would truly serve its purpose in my life. This is one topic that can be taken several ways, good or bad. I decided to use it as a positive and to my advantage. When you break down these statements, "should have, could have, and would have," they all describe situations of how the past could have been different.

I was brought up to believe you should not dwell on the past or the future but to make the most of the present. There is one person who used these statements more than anyone else I know, and his name is Bob, my stepfather. If I had to give an award for my favorite of them all, he would get the trophy. How ironic that Bob would be the one who. Because when I heard his stories of the past, I sometimes thought he was hypocritical, but I did not let him know this as I listened. Regardless of my thoughts, which were definitely judgmental, good things were to come with the formation of my perspective on the topic. This would become the catalyst of developing an optimistic mindset. One that I prefer to have over being pessimistic any day of the week. Put this all into a blender and what you will get is that each person can look deep into the past of individuals to learn. He was someone I was forced to learn from as we occasionally sat in the basement and caught a game together. He was a big San Antonio Spurs fan, and during that time they were one of the premier teams. Between the time when I attended high school and graduated from college, they won four NBA world championships.

Now I was not intentionally looking to learn from Bob's past decisions or lack thereof, but there would be valuable lessons to come out of listening to him share his stories. By the way, listening is an art form, and it is a reason we have been blessed with two ears and one mouth. We should listen two times more than speaking. It is also worth noting that it is okay to make mistakes; it is one of the reasons pencils have erasers. I have never asked him about his intentions in sharing the stories, but I would bet he wanted me to be better than him, and for that I am thankful. A wise man once told me something profound on the ability to learn from others.

> "A fool will learn from his own mistakes, and a smart individual will learn from the mistakes of others."
>
> — JAMES SURACE

When you decipher the difference between should, could, and would, the general rule is you would use a *should* statement more for recommendation or advice. The statement I remember most along this context was, "I *should* have finished school." It was because of this I made a vow with myself that I would complete school no matter what gets thrown my way and make sure to avoid saying this to my children in the future. In my household, graduating from high school, let alone college, was not the norm. But someone had to break this cycle, and I happened to be the first one to get a high school diploma and college degree. More than anything, my goal was to inspire the next generation that it can be done. Like most who have gone on to be the first to accomplish this in their family, we wear this as a badge of honor. For me, that statement inspired me to see things through.

Now when the statement *could* is used, usually the underlining meaning has to do with possibilities. The thought of possibilities on what could be used to keep me up at night. I used to imagine what I could do if I became a professional athlete. I would envision how much better life would be for my family, along with the impact to inspire those within my community. The statement I remember hearing most along this context was,

"I could have played in the NBA if I would have . . ." and hearing this I would make another vow to not repeat this same type of statement. Now I was cut from my high school basketball team not once but twice, so the only alternative way I thought I would be able to go pro was through playing football in the NFL. I made sure to exhaust all things I knew at that time to get to this level and to keep my vow. I thought about how it must feel to be haunted by thinking about what you could have done, and because of this I would be okay with the result no matter the outcome.

The statement I remember most used for *would* have involves imagining results. I heard the following statement more than a handful of times, usually while watching a San Antonio Spurs game: "I would have been the next Tim Duncan; I was the LeBron James of my time if only I would have stayed in school that would be me." At the time I thought Bob was reminiscent as he would often tell me about all his trophies. It appeared he wanted to prove how good he was back in his day. Still to this day, I never saw the trophies to prove it, and him being a good man I do not think he was lying about his accolades. I, however, doubted he would have had the same impact as Duncan or James, even though I never witnessed him play. I made sure to let him know of this in a polite way, of course. It was fun watching him get excited when I would challenge him on whether he would have been as good. I am a natural trash-talker, compliments of my environment, so it was no problem to get the conversation going. Now I know this was not right of me as you should not judge as we do not know what one is capable of, especially when you have the most high power on your side.

Around this same time is when I would really start to think about Ohio's motto, which states, "With God all things are possible" and discover its origin is from the verse in Matthew 19:26. It was because of hearing this statement and scripture I would gain confidence in what was possible on my athletic journey. If you ask anyone who grew up with me, they will tell you confidence is not something I lacked. Now of all these individuals, not one of them would know where it came from. For the first thirty-five years of my life, I did not know the source either. I thought it was from watching how my mother went about things. But I would learn about the source as I started to do inner research in the dark hours before sunrise. This is what I like to refer to as deep discovery about yourself. In Proverbs 2:4 it states, "If thou sleekest her as silver, and searchest for her as for hid treasures;" with the precept in Jeremiah 29:13: "And ye shall seek me, and find me, when ye shall search for me with all your heart." What I was able to find out about myself is that my confidence was a result of two of my favorite scriptures: Proverbs 14:26: "In the fear of the Lord is strong confidence: and his children shall have a place of refuge," and Ephesians 3:12: "In whom we have boldness and access with confidence by the faith of him."

Confidence is the ticket to get in the arena and prove what one is capable of. Once you step into the arena, the next step one must take to cement that confidence is putting in the work. Look around to any profession and study what those who are at the top one percent have as their main character trait: confidence. You will find that they have all invested a lot of valuable time in their craft. That time investment led to their confidence. There more you invest the more confident you will become in whatever it is that you do. When you take repetitive action toward something, you develop courage and confidence. Simply put, your confidence is equivalent to your work ethic. The cool thing about this perspective is that anyone can put the work in to become more confident, but the reality is there will always be a good number who will skip this step with the hopes of being in the top one percent. I believe people who settle for achieving extraordinary things demonstrate a lack of confidence. Now I do not know the amount of time Bob put into his craft, but if I had to bet, it was not enough to perform at the level he thought of himself.

One of the best professional tips I can give someone having become a part of the top one percent in my field of choice is to pay the price and *do not* take shortcuts. There is no reason to take shortcuts with the time we will all have on this journey of life. The average person will have 630,000 hours in their life, and all you have to do is invest 10,000 (1.5 percent) hours into your craft to become a professional in your field of choice and be compensated in the top one percent. Now as you can imagine at the time, I did not have this perspective, but it was inherited over time, and I wish to encourage you to use this to your advantage in your endeavors.

Do not waste time on could have, should have, or would have moments; live your life with no regrets. When it is all said and done, I hope you are not part of the many that will say, "I wish I would have done more." I implore you to squeeze every ounce of greatness within you till the clock runs out and live your life on purpose. I owe Bob a great deal of credit for helping me to create this type of perspective. There is a good chance if he was not in my life I would not have carefully thought about these scenarios. Bob, when you read this, I want you to know you are all right in my eyes. All those talks were necessary, although I did not realize it at the time. I can assure you that not one of them fell on deaf ears. The impact of sharing your story will spread further than you can imagine. I appreciate you for being there for me and showing up during precious times of my life. You made an impact on my life, and for that I forever thankful.

Bob, me, and my mom during my senior night

Challenge #9 I challenge you to learn from other people experiences and document things you wish to avoid. *What are some experiences you have learned from? I would love to hear about it. If you are willing to share, please use the hashtag #YCDI.*

Chapter Ten
IT'S NOT WHAT YOU KNOW, IT'S WHO YOU KNOW

When I was coming to the final lap of graduating college, there is a famous saying I remember hearing on what was to come as I entered the workforce. Now I can assure you my goal was to find a way to postpone this milestone event as long as I could so most of the time, I would zone out the instructors. During my senior year, the majority of my instructors offered a good amount of unsolicited advice on which type of employment one should look to obtain. Let me add that the information was helpful for the average person, but little did they know I had aspirations to not be average in life.

When I speak on the word *average*, I am not talking about the usual vanity of status, money, or fame. My view on avoiding the pursuit of an average life has always revolved around the amount of impact I can have during my time here on earth. Just hearing the word *average* itself is one I despise, and I usually end up having an unsettling feeling inside. The idea of pursuing anything average, especially in a career, and dedicating time to something revolving around just making money would be unfulfilling. Jobs come in all shapes and sizes, and I had my fair share of jobs prior to graduating, which gave me somewhat of an idea of what I wanted in a career. One thing for sure from every job I held is that I absolutely knew what I did not want in a career. I did not want to be told what I am worth. I did not want to work in a factory setting. I did not want to work in a setting where I would be held back due to tenure, race, or religion. I did not want to be the only minority in the place as I had already paid my dues being in these types of uncomfortable settings. These were the top things I looked to avoid.

Initially, I was looking for a job, not necessarily a career. I define a job as "just over broke," and like most I did not want to remain broke. I wanted to eventually have the ability to control my income as an intrapreneur prior to becoming an entrepreneur. My desired vehicle would come with a prerequisite where I had the ability to control my income along with all the things I looked to avoid. Let me add that money is not everything, but if used correctly good things could come from obtaining a good amount. We all know someone who worships money and material things. Usually, the outcome for these individuals if they refuse to change is a life of nothing but emptiness. I hope when you look in the mirror that person is not you. If it is you, I encourage you to reevaluate your priorities in life. 1 Timothy 6:10 states a common teaching: "For the love of money is the root of all evil: which while some coveted after, they have erred from the faith, and pierced themselves through with many sorrows." It details the impact that the love of money can have on us.

For the individuals who are studied, you know that money is a defense. As it says in Ecclesiastes 7:12, "For wisdom is a defence, and money is a defence: but the excellency of knowledge is that wisdom giveth life to them that have it." The advice here is to pursue it wisely. I have learned that not all work is equal and the experience thereof likewise. One should choose their work wisely, regardless of compensation. I can truly say that I have met some happy people with low pay and miserable people with high pay. The dichotomy between the two is based on each individual and their set of priorities.

Let me tell you about the work experience I had up to this point in my life. Each job I held consisted of being paid hourly. Most of my employment was around things I was able to excel at and genuinely enjoyed. Diane gave me my first official job at Redeemer Iglesias Crisis Center where I had the pleasure of serving kids during the summer program of the outreach center. This would be the same place that provided summer lunch to all the kids in the neighborhood, monthly meals to the community, clothes to those in need, and food to my mother when we were in need, so I always felt the need to give back to this place. The day I was able to make a pretty sizable donation, it meant the world to me.

Giving Diane donation for Redeemer Crisis Center

The best part of this day was showing my wife and daughter this staple to the community where I grew up and the place that made serving others meaningful to me. It was nothing like helping serve on the line during the monthly community meal.

It always humbled me and made me appreciate things, even when I thought at the time that I did not have much. Now I will not bore you with all the jobs I held, but I must tell you about a few. The job I held at the Coca-Cola factory the summer of my junior year was quite an experience. It did not last long as I found out very quick, I was not built for the factory life. It is something about being in what they called a "plant" that reminded me of plantation work. The image of individuals walking around perimeters, overseeing things with those flashing red lights and alarm sounds throughout the facility when production was negatively affected, I will always remember. Not to mention having to get on the road at 5:00 a.m. to report to work. All this for five dollars more per hour than anything I held previously. Hopefully, they do not remember how much money I cost them for slowing down their lines, but I know it was a pretty penny. I came into that job as some cocky individual who thought he could manage anything. Boy was I humbled. The highlight of this experience was having Jamoni Robinson, my college roommate and football teammate who also worked there with me, hysterically laugh at me each day as I screwed things up. He was able to take in the view of me causing a domino effect of plastic bottles falling all over the place while both machines I had to manage got clogged at the same time as I ran around like a chicken with no head. His line was cake as he called it, but mine not so much. It was a sight to see, and we still laugh about this experience till this day.

At this job is where I would learn about the importance of synchronicity in daily productivity while maintaining your sanity. There was a moment where I had to ask myself if I was willing to trade for my sanity for fifteen dollars per hour, and the answer was no. It definitely showed in my performance on the job, which resulted in the production manager and me coming to an agreement that it was not the best fit. There was, however, another job I had prior to graduating, and this was the first time I would stare at the clock. I still remember the many days when I could not wait until the shift was over while working in the lumber department of Home Depot. This was the most lonely job I held as I did not have much interaction with customers. The occasional wood cutting got old really quick, and every day I could not wait to catch the RTA home after my shift. To say this was the longest summer job would be an understatement. Now this is no knock on any of the employers or anyone in the line of work mentioned. My overall view regarding any workplace environment is that regardless of the type of career or job and whether or not something of significance is achieved in the workplace, it still will not be enough for when my heart stops beating, and judgement day comes.

Whenever someone makes a statement such as, "When my heart stops beating, people will know I was here," I can assure you they plan to do big things. Now just saying something like this will not be the reason it becomes a reality. The work must be done over a lifetime. The first time I omitted this statement I was wet behind the ears and not even a teenager. Those around me at the time absolutely thought I was full of it. I am still curious as to what my professor thought when I said the same thing to him and several others throughout my life. Maybe I will never know what they thought or how they felt at the time.

Most might think it was all about some self-fulfilling prophecy, but my purpose in life has nothing to do with me. It has always been bigger than me, and anyone else who will grace this place we call earth.

Now I must give credit to my higher learning as they did a great job of preparing us all for what they called the "real world." I can recall the etiquette classes for luncheons, public speaking sessions, resume building assignments, and countless other simulated experiences involving situations that would all eventually come in handy. The kid from the hood of Cleveland sure needed this as well as other types of preparation. I was not naive to the fact that the majority of individuals I would encounter during my future search of employment on the surface would not have much in common with me or look like me, so it was a must to take the preparation seriously. I can assure you I would not use this as an excuse either, unlike some who choose to do so.

For the attention to detail placed on the curriculum prepared, I had a good amount of appreciation for it as I would learn that in the future it would help serve me. I hear a lot of people make statements nowadays that college is pointless, but I would like to challenge anyone who has completed higher education that if you look back over all the things you were taught, I am sure you can find at least one thing of value. Now was the price of obtaining that piece of paper truly worth it? I will let you decide that for yourself. But mine led to a greater return of investment (ROI). We can leave out the cost for books, which I think was the biggest swindle in the history of higher learning. I still cannot believe we let these institutions get away with overpricing these items at an insane amount to then resale for less than half the amount originally purchased and then watch them resell at the full price the following year. Going through this proves I did not know much about the system as I was voluntarily taken advantage of. If I were to go back, I would have exercised the title of this chapter a little more to get a better deal on books.

I learned that the "who you know" part of the saying is the key to getting in certain doors. Learning this allowed me to develop the perspective that it is also not wise to gossip about other people as it is best to discuss goals, family, dreams, ideas, personal development, and solutions when in conversation. Most know it is always an exception to the rule when talking about people, and in this case, I will support that notion. The day when I drove from Cleveland to Alliance, Ohio, to meet with Mrs. Doak, the head of career services department, one year after I had graduated proves this to be true. I was embarrassed at the time of the meeting. Although she did not know it, I promise you I had the intention of never showing it. She sat me down and did the best she could do to guide me.

This was at a time when I desperately needed employment. After the departure of my first position post grad and having one year of successful employment with one of the largest banks in the US at Wells Fargo Financial, I found myself in a tough place. I was starting to get behind on bills after pursing tryouts to become a professional athlete. My car at the time was my prized possession, and GMAC made sure to remind me if I did not get payments in very soon, they were going to come repossess the car I was leasing. I took those phone calls seriously as it was not that long ago since I had a car repossessed. Let me tell you, there is nothing like waking up and coming out to "your whip," and seeing it is no longer there. If you ever want to get back on your feet, then simply miss two car payments (lol). This is one of the best pieces of humble pie you can eat. Now none of this was disclosed to Mrs. Doak, but she did live up to her commitment of her role to connect me with some alumni whom I might know.

We spoke for a good time, and I must share how she had a special way of making me feel good about the future. Her motherly aura made all the difference in my ability to maintain my mixed emotions at the time. I came into her office scared, not knowing what was next, and left feeling like everything was going to be all right. Once we got around to what I was looking for, she was able to make a few recommendations of where I should apply. The icing on the cake was her promise to me that she would do her best to ensure I would connect with the employers. This was the first time I had someone from my college make a promise to me that I actually believed.

We would eventually narrow down the choices to where I would apply, and the final list comprised of three listings. One of which was a financial service company job opening. The former student who listed the job played baseball, and the job description fit the narrative. I followed her advice and applied to the job. A few days later I was called in for an interview, which turned out to be more than a job; it would eventually become a life-changing opportunity. I'm forever thankful to Nick Zangardi for viewing my resume and opening this door for me. My life would not be the same had he not. I will never be able to repay him. The day I passed the exam to become a licensed insurance professional, I made it very clear to him he had no idea what was about to happen. I was confident in making such a statement simply based on belief.

Belief is a critical component in achieving what the world defines as success. Research shows that the highest levels of human performance are empowered by the deepest levels of belief. I had strong belief in everything Nick told me about the opportunity. I was attracted to the possibility of making some money and would still get to work out and wait for the call to go show my athletic talents in hopes of making a professional football roster. I got a call from a scout, but it was about four years too late. I was having dinner at McAlister's Deli with my then business partner at the time and our families. It was a cold winter day in Indiana, and I did not recognize the number, so I let it go to voicemail. This was a pivotal moment in my life; it was the exclamation of completing a move to a new state for a business opportunity. That day we just finished getting settled after the move. When I listened to the voicemail after checking out from the restaurant, I knew that was confirmation from the Most High that I was making the right decision and that the NFL opportunity I desired was right in my hands.

It would be with this company where I would learn things about what it took to be a true servant leader. The day I came in for my initial interview, I knew this was not the average opportunity. Yes, the office was the most fast paced (to this day, I have never seen anyone walk down a hall faster than Vasu) and best one I had ever seen. The people were young in age and in thinking, very nice and relatable. The smell was fresh, and I felt comfortable. Here is where for the first time in a workplace setting I would develop relationships that were bigger than profits. The most prized relationships taught me about the importance of personal development in the areas of spirit, mind, and body along with how great relationships are commensurate to great results. These are just a few key ingredients one should follow in the quest to build a successful business. One of the most paramount examples of the statement "It's who you know" is how the apostles viewed things with their relationship with Christ in Acts 15:11: "But we believe that through the grace of the Lord Jesus Christ we shall be saved, even as they." This magnifies that it is not what you know that counts; it is who you know! I would like to encourage you to intentionally surround yourself with those who bring out the best in you, not the stress in you. Every day you have an opportunity to surround yourself with people who will help you grow. Good people will help you stay connected to the vine and challenge you when you are doing things that might disconnect you. Embrace those who will tell you want you need to hear, and stay away from people who do not want to see you succeed in life. I have found that if you look for the following qualities in someone, you will blossom into the best version of yourself.

Challenge #10 I challenge you to be intentional with your relationship-building and look for people who can add value with high influence. *Have you been able to open doors based upon who you know? If so, I would love to hear about it. If you are willing to share, please use the hashtag #YCDI.*

Chapter Eleven

WHAT'S THE DIFFERENCE BETWEEN THEM AND YOU?

My mother once presented this question to me when I was a teenager. My response at the time was "nothing" as I knew she was just trying to teach me another lesson on perseverance. Honestly, I had a good number of firsthand experiences watching her endure a lot of things throughout her life, so I felt there was no reason to debate her on the topic. Yes, I was a knucklehead and actually tried debating with my mother a few times. This was during the teenage years where I started to challenge her thinking. But this one right here, "What's the difference between them and you?" was pretty powerful. I do not know if she understood the magnitude of what this question would do for my mindset.

I have thought very deep about the question and resolved with the notion that all men have several things in common. First, starting with how we all enter the world the same way right out of our mother's womb. Contrary to what some might believe, there is no man or woman who came into this earth without bearing a physical mother and father. From the greatest man to ever walk earth to the most recent infant born at the same time you are reading this book, we all share this commonality. Believe it or not, there was once a man and woman who both got excited enough to come together, and you appeared sometime later, roughly about nine months after that encounter. Lucky you, they had that encounter at the correct time or else you would be hanging out in a sack or who knows where. If you Google the odds of being born, you will find there is a four hundred trillion to one chance of having life [6]. For this very reason, I am always reminded of how lucky we all are.

Now in all my years on earth, I have come to understand some people never got a chance to meet their biological parents. This must be one of the hardest things to cope with in life. I can partially relate to this as I had to learn after thirty-five years the man who I thought was my biological dad turned out to be someone I never got a chance to meet as he passed away before I came to this understanding. John Jordan lived to be seventy-five and passed away peacefully on March 30, 2015. According to his obituary, he was a loving father, brother, grandfather, great-grandfather, uncle, and friend to many. Still to this day, I have not met anyone with the Jordan name whom I am related to. As you can imagine, I went through a slight depression at the time after seeing my ancestry results. I tried to mask the feelings of what I was going through inside, but after doing some self-reflecting I could not hide it anymore. The first person who noticed that I was struggling with finding out the news was my wife. My assistant also found out and I eventually felt compelled to share the information with my entire team. I wanted to use my story to encourage someone to appreciate knowing and having their parents. Maybe I would have responded in a negative way had my mother revealed this information to me earlier in life. Regardless, it was hard coping with the feeling of thinking your entire life was a lie. I can usually handle hearing tough news, but this was a hard pill to swallow, and the day it was revealed to me is one I will never forget.

April 4, 2019, was the day my mother surprised me for my birthday with a special visit at my business all the way from Cleveland, Ohio, to Indianapolis, Indiana. I was excited for her to finally see me in action after all these years. It would end up becoming one of the most productive and eventful days of my life. I would start my day as usual at 4:00 a.m. with the help of my "opportunity clock," immediately followed by hitting my knees in prayer before using the restroom, then brushing my teeth and getting my system going by drinking my probiotics down with some lemon water. This morning my coffee would even turn out perfect with the letter *C* naturally forming in the foam. I got comfortable in my reading chair around 4:30 a.m. and took in some much-needed internal development. I would rise around 6:30 a.m. to get ready for the gym and leave my house at 6:45 a.m. I arrived at my gym by 7:00 a.m. to have one of the best workouts of the year. In my mind I thought it might have been old man strength as I would laugh at myself for the thought on the ride home. The pump lasted longer than normal, so I must have been really tapping into endorphins. I left the gym around 8:00 a.m. just in time to get home and shower then hit the road. The drive was smooth, traffic flowed to my liking, and I was able to arrive at my office five minutes earlier than expected.

Those who know me know I do not like surprises or celebrating my birthday, but this day there was a packed room full of energetic individuals who went against the grain. They all went above your typical celebration. Despite the festivities, the day was still packed with meetings, and it was during what I called our weekly "huddle" meeting my mother would make a grand entrance. At first, I did not recognize her with the blonde hair as she entered the room to surprise me, but when we left for lunch, I made sure to give her my unsolicited opinion about her hair. I have always had a straightforward relationship with my mother. She never sugarcoats anything with me, and I have always believed that gave me permission to do the same. We enjoyed a nice lunch at one of our favorite places to eat, and I made sure to remind her to lose the blonde hair. If you look up the history on blonde hair in the early Roman Empire, you will find that prostitutes were required to have yellow hair (usually wigs) as a mark of their profession. I could not have my mother out here looking like a harlot.

Surprise birthday lunch with my mother

Later that evening, we would treat my mother to a nice dinner at Seasons 52. After dinner I thought it would be convenient to make a quick trip to Costco and secure a flat-screen TV that was on sale. I could not pass up this opportunity to ensure she got rid of that old TV she had at home as it drove me crazy every time I would visit. The view on that thing was seventeen years behind, so it was absolutely time for an upgrade. Little did I know I would receive news in the car before going in the store that would really impact my view on things. I briefly shared with her my ancestry results and mentioned how it was very odd that I did not see anyone with the name Cunningham linked to me. This is where it was revealed to me that I had an entirely different biological dad, and I am not sure if there could have been a better setting for this conversation, but immediately my heart sank. Interestingly enough, she revealed to me how she had intentions to discuss this with me seventeen years earlier. I had a weird way of internalizing this information and temporarily resolved it with the notion that everything happens for a reason. It was not until I got home where it hit me, and I became very emotional just thinking about what has just happened.

I forgave my mother for holding on to this devastating information for thirty-five years and have since continued to lean on one of my favorite proverbs: "Trust in the LORD with all thine heart; and lean not unto thine own understanding" (Proverbs 3:5). I can only imagine how painful it must have been holding this in knowing there is no way the information once delivered would not hurt. I do not know why I was dealt this hand, but either way I am just happy he formed me in the womb. I was able to learn that regardless of the circumstances, it is best to never have the mentality of feeling like you have been dealt a poor hand. If you ever start to question if you are a winner or even good enough for taking on this journey we call life, remember you once won a race in a competition of a one-hundred-million-plus swim to a very important destination. You crossed that finish line to the egg first and was blessed with life. No matter what, never take this blessing of life for granted.

James Cunningham Jr, Mother and me

Yes, you can say this perspective might involve changing the way you view things. It will always be about killing our ego and pride every day. These two things hold back many in life. The biggest battles we will face in life reside within. Once you understand this, you now have an awareness of the battle. Now winning the daily battle is another story. People will count you out. They might not think you will make it or even believe in you, but I have news for you: it is up to you to determine if it will be true. Although people will count you out, remember that God will never stop counting. For anyone out there who wants to come out as a winner, I would advise you get and stay armored up. The desire to win consists of your daily actions of getting armored up. We are truly in a war each day, and knowing this is half the battle. Pity the man who is competent of this understanding yet voluntarily chooses to not do anything about it.

Challenge #11 I challenge you to identify your unique qualities and the advantages you have. *I would love to hear about them. If you are willing to share, please use the hashtag #YCDI.*

Chapter Twelve

USE THE TOWEL OR THROW IT IN, YOUR CHOICE

In most professional sports stadiums, you can find raving fans waving rally towels all around the world, especially on any given Sunday. I always found this to be interesting. Arguably the most iconic of them all is the "Terrible Towel" sported by loyal Pittsburgh Steelers fans. It is one of the most famous rally towels in sports history. The Pittsburgh Steelers were the first football team to hand out rally towels to their fans. Growing up in Cleveland, we definitely thought the color yellow was terrible, but as I paid more attention that towel grew on me. What impressed me the most was the way the fans supported their favorite team. This has a lot to do with the culture of the organization and the unique ways they go about connecting with people to allow their players to feed off their energy.

The culture of their towel is so strong, I was able to witness firsthand how it found a way to infiltrate a company where I was once invited to speak. This workplace happened to be the top financial service insurance company in all of Pittsburgh. To give you some additional details on this company, they are known to have a winning culture that could rival their hometown team, including having their very own version of the Terrible Towel. The energy in the audience that day was similar to attending a game, which made it even better. There were about five hundred people in attendance (in person and remote), so of course it was fitting to share my perspective of the infamous towel, especially being from Cleveland. I asked how many Browns fans resided in their town and a few hands were raised to my surprise. Where I went next with talking about the towel would turn around and surprise them.

I had to first acknowledge that there were men and women in the room who have all been dealt a different set of cards in life. I would follow that up with letting them know that despite where you are now and wherever you are going in the future, it is important to keep in mind how you will use the towel you have been blessed to wave. "This organization has a sacred towel that I have seen waved with pride in front of thousands of people. I want to leave you with this that in life you will go through some $%#! and how you use the towel will determine your outcome. When you go through adversity, will you use it to wipe the sweat off your head? Or will you just throw in the towel? I have a better idea! You not only can use it to wipe the sweat off; it can also be used to wipe the $%#! off yourself when you have mess to clean up. How will you use it when this happens to you? Will you wipe or just walk around with $%#! on you? We are not babies anymore. No one is coming to change your diaper when you $%#! Yourself. It's your total responsibility to clean things up. The best thing about this is that you will have individuals who will care enough to tell you when they recognize it on you. The perspective I want to leave you with is that you have a duty and obligation to not walk around smelling, thinking, talking, or performing like $%#!"

Speaking to Arias Organization

This towel perspective happens to be one of many I choose to live by, no matter the circumstances. I learned about this lesson my very first fist fight in my front yard at the age of nine. I was slapped across the side of my face so hard I could hardly hear out of my ear. It took hours before I was able to clearly hear again. In the moment, I literally thought it was going to be permanent. I will never forget that it hurt so bad I ran home from the bully in our neighborhood, who chased me to my house along with his mother that followed him. When I got in the house, I felt very secure but was immediately given my first ultimatum by my mother. She told me, "You either go back outside and kick his you know what, or I'm going to whoop you're a** myself."

I chose to go back outside because this woman was a professional butt-whooper, and I was positive that getting a whooping from her would definitely hurt a lot worse. If you were raised with this type of discipline, I am sure you would have done the same thing. That day I did not throw in the towel and learned the importance of standing up for myself. When the fight was over, I was victorious. From that moment on I was not afraid of bullies. I would go on to become the individual in school who would stick up for others when the bully would pick on them. We will all have those fight-or-flight moments in life. Simply put, we can all throw in our towel or use it wisely. There will be more than enough opportunities for us all throughout our journey in life to use it the right way. I encourage you to use yours to always clean things up and never throw it in.

We all have the ability to be victorious. It is inside all of us, but sadly enough there are far too many individuals who allow it to never come to fruition. I have seen people allow the opinion of others to dictate how they will use their towel. Friends might tell you what you want to hear, but your allies will tell you what you need to hear. No matter the difference, it's always best to surround yourself with people who want to see you use your towel in the right manner. I would strongly suggest that you embrace this concept and understand that only you can use your towel. I can guarantee you that if you throw in your towel, you will not win. Regardless of what winning means to your life, it will always have its own language and does not allow you to bull$%#! your way through.

Life sure has a unique way of shaping our perspective on this subject. Who would have ever thought about the four-letter word in this context. Yes, it comes in all shapes and sizes. It could be big or little $%#! There is no way around the reality that we all will encounter it. Keeping a clean perspective will allow you to use your towel over the long haul on the quest to achieve all that you desire in life. Perspective will help fuel you along the way. What I have found out in life and over the course of my journey as an entrepreneur is that most people will throw in the towel to win a sale. When the first wave of adversity hits, most people throw the towel in. Do not be most people! Be uncommon and never get comfortable sitting in your own $%#! Can comfort buy your dreams? I would bet if you made it this far in the book, the answer is no. In the process, you will have to find a zone just make sure your zone is never comfort. If you have a vision, it will require you to exercise this concept, when necessary, on the journey.

Challenge #12 I challenge you to never throw the towel in and always look for ways that you can use it. *How have you used your towel throughout life? I would love to hear about it. If you are willing to share, please use the hashtag #YCDI.*

Chapter Thirteen
LIVING IN 4D

The first television I ever watched was on a 1984 Magnavox color TV, and it was not that much of a difference from the black-and-white displays we had around. Fast-forward to the current times, and we can now operate in a virtual world. Not sure how many people saw that coming, but back in the 1980s we were pretty content with the picture quality we had. But like most things, it is a must that all things evolve.

Now when cable entertainment entered the scene, it was good timing for me personally. The most positive thing that came out of it was keeping me out of the streets. I remember the day when the "cable man" came to install our box. I probably annoyed him with all the questions I had about the process of installation. If I could go back, I would have asked him if he was aware that those boxes had secret installed cameras and microphones. I was just a curious kid who was excited about having the luxury to watch some cool shows that would interest me. It did not take long for me to realize my sisters were just as excited, so we had to immediately establish a rule for who would have control on the remote. We decided whoever got the remote first (excluding our mother, who always had first dibs) decided on what show to watch. Whenever I would beat my sisters to the remote, I would enjoy all my favorite shows on Fox kids and Nickelodeon in peace, including *X-Men*, *Teenage Mutant Ninja Turtles*, *WWF*, and *Scooby Doo*, although we would collectively enjoy the likes of BET together.

The quality of the modern-day television viewing pleasure comes with plentiful options to choose from, and there is no longer a need for a big cable box. Just like the picture quality we choose for our liking, it is just as important to make daily decisions that are best for our lives. The quality of every daily decision we make is imperative to how things will be for you in the future. It is estimated that the average adult makes more than 35,000 decisions everyday [7]. Some start the day with hitting their knees in prayer while others go right to opening up their device to scroll. Regardless of how you start your day, it is imperative to win the day. What does this mean? It is recognizing that our daily choices are the difference between what our present and future will look like. The cost of our good choices and bad choices will reflect at different times. Our daily habits can work for us or against us. When you decide the type of person you want to be, your daily habits will prove if you want to win each day. If the system you create aligns with your goals, you will catapult and reach the destination you desire. For those who desire to win, you must do the things you need to do, whether you feel like it or not, before you get to do the things you want. This is what you call prioritizing to "W.I.N." This acronym simply means doing "What's Important Now." The cool thing is if you win the day consecutively enough, you will develop a winning streak. Every soul that still has the breath of life can set goals and check them off before completion of the day at sundown.

On the flip side, I am willing to bet that you will not accomplish any of the goals you do not set. The time it takes to plan your work and work your plan each day is less costly than winging it. No matter where you are, it is absolutely necessary to identify the daily habits that have the highest return of investment (ROI) on your daily work, then prioritize them from most important to least. I highly suggest you spend the majority of your time doing the habits and activities that will give you the best ROI. If you are going to invest in something, make sure it is more on assets than liabilities. The best investment will always be in yourself, and at the top of the list I encourage you to not underestimate the power of prayer.

For the majority of my life, I was missing this component. Most of my life it was uncomfortable praying as I did not know what to say. To say I was blessed to be in a workplace environment where I could get wisdom and understanding on something of this nature is an understatement. One day in 2009, I had enough courage to ask James Surace how should I pray. His answer was simple to understand as I was instructed to acknowledge, confess, give thanks, and ask for supplication. I followed his advice, and the outcome was that I became more comfortable with doing it. Now at the time I did not realize that Christ, better known as "Our Saviour" or Yashaya in

Hebrew (see *Strong's* translation H3467), gave us all clear instructions on how to pray in Matthew 6:5–15. At this time in my life, I was too lazy to open a Bible, which is part of the reason Jim gave me a copy. I still have it and will always keep it as a reminder. I was once part of the many individuals who claim to be a follower of Christ but never read the Bible. Did you know that of the over two billion Christians in the world, less than 30 percent will ever read through the entire Bible? Studies show that 86 percent of Americans claim to be Christian, and most will never read the book [8]. Regardless of what you believe, I encourage you to read the writings for yourself. In 2 Timothy 3:16 it says, "All scripture is given by inspiration of God, and is profitable for doctrine, for reproof, for correction, for instruction in righteousness." I needed correction and was looking to get instruction for once in my life, so I decided to read for myself. Once I started to read, it felt like a weight was lifted off my shoulders. This all came from a seed that was planted by Jim. I just had to water that seed. It is not often you cross paths with a leader in the business sector who has all that a man could ever want in his business endeavors but decides to use his platform as his ministry to impact the ordinary man or woman at a higher level than just generating revenue. I was impressed with the character he displayed from the very first day I met him. He is the first servant leader and philanthropist I met in business who was a living example of what the Bible defines as a good man. I can draft an entire book on the priceless things he taught me over the years under his leadership, but for the sake of the subject I will stick to a few principles about daily decisions.

The first lesson I learned from him is that if you do not control your calendar, your calendar will control you. What he taught us all is that time is measured in minutes, and life is measured in moments. How you invest your time will determine your return of investment. Time can only be invested once, so it must be invested wisely. Not all time is created equal. Time is relative, and we are subjected to it; therefore, we must make the most of every minute and every moment. It reads in 2 Peter 3:8, "But, beloved, be not ignorant of this one thing, that one day [is] with the Lord as a thousand years, and a thousand years as one day." The Lord is not subject to time like you and me, in fact he can bend it. When God comes to earth, time is bent!

At the height of my career in financial services, if you were to look at my weekly calendar, you would find that every day was planned—all the way down to each minute of the day. This skill I learned from Marcus Smith who, a decade later after banging my head against the wall, would teach me how to effectively build a daily routine revolved around intentional growth and maximizing one hundred sixty-eight hours each week. We developed a bulletproof growth formula that will serve anyone looking to become the best version of themselves. I learned over the years if you want to have growth, it will all come down to blocking out time for important and urgent things over less important and non-urgent matters. I must admit that it took quite some time to understand this concept and determine what action items aligned best with my goals. But once this was determined, I experienced growth in every area of my life.

The best part of planning your work is that it will allow for less error and more productivity. After you plan your work, you must work your plan if you want to see progress. Sadly, most individuals prefer to delay obedience to a daily routine, which is in turn disobedience to growth itself. Growth requires consistency, and this consistency beats intensity each day of the week. Most people do not get what they want in life because they do not take time to really figure out what they want, and their approach is inconsistent. Once the approach is consistent and the decision to pay the price is made daily, then is when *you can* expect a good ROI. As long as you continue to do the work necessary, it then only becomes a matter of time before you start to check off goals. Please note anything worth doing has no discount on the price; you must pay the price in full. But guess what? There will be no balance. I tried looking for balance and unfortunately never found it. I would love to spare you the time and let you know that you will not find it either on the road to achieving greatness. What I did find was that I would need to blend things. Check out how I found ways to blend my priorities:

TYPICAL DAY
4:00 AM – 6:30 AM – Wake up: Pray, Proverbs and Book, LLJ, Daily Maxwell, Journal
7:00 AM – 8:30 AM – Workout/Podcast or Audible/ Call Mom on drive home
8:30 AM – 9:00 AM – Shower, shake and coffee, drive to office
9:00 AM – 9:30 AM – "CHAMPIONS" meeting
9:30 AM – 10:00 AM – Webinar
10:00 AM – 10:30 AM – F6 Development or Bullpen
10:30 AM – 11:00 AM – P6 Development
11:00 AM – 12:00 PM – RELEASE & PROMOTION MEETINGS/ Review ICM Reports/ Interviews
12:00 PM – 1:30 PM – Lunch meeting (1 on 1 or group) with Staff/ CMC (Simon & Marcus)
1:30 PM – 2:00 PM – Pregame/Review Financials and Payroll/Meet with PR or Pipeline/ Zoom Q&A/Roleplay
2:00 PM – 3:00 PM – Team Huddle (Leadership Development) or *Coaching Calls*
3:00 PM – 3:30 PM – Chiropractor
3:30 PM – 4:00 PM – CHECK IN WITH DIRECT REPORTS & "Thankful Walk" with Dogs
4:00 PM – 4:30 PM – Pipeline & Social Media Mgmt (Strategize with ACM)
4:30 PM – 5:00 PM – *SGA Zoom Meeting* or Study CMC notes
5:00 PM – 6:00 PM – *Email Mgmt*/ To-Do-List/ Starting 10 & Colleges/Review *"flash report"* – VIRTUAL RIDEOUTS (VR)+ FILM
6:00 PM – 7:30 PM – Track Practice or Cardio & (VR)
7:30 PM – 8:00 PM – Book: YOU CAN DO IT
8:00 PM – 10:00 PM – Date Night with Wife or QT with Family or Dinner with PR/ Gratitude - Devotional/Read then sleep

Whatever the size of your goals, big or small, it is important to note that God will not honor goals that do not honor him.

Follow the advice of King Solomon about work: "Commit thy way unto the Lord; trust also in him; and he shall bring it to pass" (Psalm 37:5). And remember what Yashaya said in Matthew 19:26: "With men this is impossible; but with God all things are possible." Never put a period where God puts a comma. I encourage you as you make plans to pray on them and note that a God idea is better than a good idea. You will not always be motivated, but you can always stay disciplined. Treat discipline like you love it, even when you dislike it. Live a 4D life and understand that **daily discipline determines destiny**. We all are capable of making small changes that lead to big results. It all starts with daily choices that impact who we are today and the person we wish to become. Once you decide the type of person you want to be, it's up to you to prove it to yourself. The things you do daily is a direct reflection of the answer to whatever it is you decide. Allow your daily habits to compound in your favor. Adopt this way of living, and go against the grain of traditional living. Focus on what you can control each day, not the future which is not promised, nor the day that already passed. Our destiny is already determined by our discipline in what we do each day.

Challenge #13 I challenge you to audit what you do each day and find ways to make better decisions. *What daily disciplines do you have that bring positive returns? I would love to hear about them. If you are willing to share, please use the hashtag #YCDI.*

Chapter Fourteen

HOW MUCH DO YOU HAVE IN YOUR CUP?

In 2010, I learned about the importance of water consumption thanks to Jim introducing it to our organization. Another reason why my respect for him increased. I started to realize he truly did care about our overall well-being. Our senior leadership team at the time went on a quest to learn about *The 7 Pillars of Health* by Don Colbert. Although I was a knucklehead (Bulldog, thanks for reminding me of this!) and came into some of the meetings with a banana and yogurt, which drove Marcus crazy. This was the first book that I intentionally took an interest in learning how to have better health. We covered each area outlined in the book: water, sleep, stress, food, exercise, detoxification, and nutrients. My favorite chapter was on water, and one of the first things I realized about myself is that for the majority of my life I consumed an inadequate amount of water. At this time in my life, most of my daily liquid consumption consisted of coffee, juice, iced tea, Kool-Aid, pop (the real name for you soda lovers), and the occasional Corona with a lime around noon on Sundays. Now, I am not promoting this way of living by any means, as you know there are many ways to consume liquid. And if you choose to consume alcohol it should be responsibly and in moderation. As you can see, I was lacking the most important liquid of them all. The funny thing is that I knew this was an issue, yet I proudly made excuses why it was not a priority in my liquid consumption. Here is typical response I would make to the individuals who would call me out (they are the ones who really care for you) about not drinking enough water: "Well, water is in this liquid, so technically I am drinking water." We can both agree this is a simple response and was very foolish of me.

Water was not the most important liquid in my life at the time, but as I learned about its importance for the body, I decided to make a change in my routine. It was imperative to get serious about getting healthier and being more intentional about what I put in my body as I was now a father. Everyone always says they would die for their kids, but would you get healthy for them? If you have someone depending on you and you disregard your input, I think it is selfish of you to not take care of your temple. Since then, I have started my mornings with water before anything else. This change would open up my thinking one early morning as I poured water in my glass. I had the analogy we all have heard of "half empty or half full" come to me in a different way. It clicked with me that it does not matter if the glass is half-empty or half-full, just make sure you are the one pouring. Yes, you will be responsible for pouring a lot of things in life, but this is what I call the best pouring you can do: *pouring into yourself so you can pour into others*. Now just because someone decides to pour into themselves does not mean it is enough as we must also pour an adequate amount of the necessary things at the right time of day. This understanding of properly taking care of my temple led to helping me improve how I went about pouring into myself. See, each person who will ever breathe will have the sole responsibility to take care of themselves at some point in life. When it comes to leadership, I learned an invaluable lesson during my tenure in financial services that it is absolutely necessary when leading others to first fill your cup up with the correct amount for those you will need to fill up. You must make the daily deposit before having human interaction with those you lead or else you run the risk of not having enough to pour out when the opportunity presents itself.

I was first exposed to the idea of pouring into myself after attending a funeral for a coworker who committed suicide by blowing his brains out with a double barrel shotgun. That evening of events is one I will never forget. The news traveled fast from Columbus to Cleveland, Ohio, that one of our peers was in a suicidal attempt. This was a young man who had a bright future ahead, but only if he continued to run the race of life. That day in attendance of his funeral and seeing his family grieve inspired me to look at what I had in my cup. I saw firsthand what happens when you voluntarily choose to not adequately fill yourself up and the negative impact it will have on those you love. I can assure you those who voluntarily follow you expect you to never be in this type of situation. If you have the habit of not pouring into yourself, then whether you like it or not, you are hurting your people. **A question** every "leader" should ask themselves: **Are your people better off or worse from their time with you?** Hopefully, the answer is yes for you. If for whatever reason you are unsure, I can assure you that if you focus on serving yourself and then others, you will be confident in the answer. Fun fact: Did you know the term *leader* is only mentioned eleven times in the King James Bible (Old Testament, Apocrypha, New Testament) while the term servant is mentioned 927 times! When I learned this, my perspective on leading changed from leading to serving.

Here is the reality check we all need to understand, the most important person you will ever lead is yourself. The highest level of personal development comes from serving yourself first. Regardless of your title, position, tenure, or accolades, none of these things will help solve the problems of those who look to you for leadership. Every person you will have the privilege to serve has problems they need help solving. As a leader, it is imperative you help them find solutions. I can also attest that sometimes you will encounter those who do not want to focus on solutions and growth. This is still no excuse to not fill yourself up properly. On the contrary, it is worth noting if you are a person who gets easily offended from someone being real with you in the attempt to help solve your problem, you rob yourself of the opportunity to experience growth. To the leaders out there, this might sound like a lot of pressure. Regardless of how it might appear to you, let me remind you that you signed up for all that you have on your plate. I am confident you can handle it all without succumbing to the pressure. Have you ever experienced an overwhelming amount of pressure from family, friends, and business at the same time?

Embrace it all, and do not run away from it. This is an opportunity to earn a degree from the University of Adversity. I would like to encourage you to learn from individuals who have overcome the same battles. This is where the cheat code awaits you to get the results you desire. The ability to save yourself headache and time is imperative with this type of approach. There is a great opportunity for us all to use others experiences to our advantage and prove how coachable we are in the process. **Another question every "leader" should ask themselves: How can I expect to grow as a better person 364 days from now if I keep doing the same thing I did 364 days ago?** The solution is always to invest in yourself. Remember, your input determines your output. Don't be like most people, who invest more into their vehicle than they do into themselves. Whatever you invest in you will see a return on. If you are not investing in yourself, do not expect to improve.

Another question every "leader" should consistently ask themselves: What investments am making into myself? If you do not invest in yourself, then there is a good chance you do not believe in yourself. Therefore, why should someone else believe in you? The other reason is because you are a sluggard. Show me how much you invested in yourself the last year and I will show you how much growth you will have in the near future. Make a commitment to yourself that there will not be any corner-cutting with your personal growth. You cannot want the extra things in life if you are not willing to go the extra mile. Most people make the excuse that they do not have time. But I know a lot of winners, and the one difference between them and those labeled as losers is how they invest their time. These same individuals see themselves as the best version of themself and strive to become that each day. Be a winner in your race of life outside the womb, and never forget you already won the one inside.

If you want to do better or win your race, then keep reading. If you have no desire for these things, stop reading and please gift this book to someone who desires growth.

Let me remind you that there is unlimited potential in you. If anyone has told you otherwise, I would advise you to avoid talking with them moving forward. I have witnessed that anyone can have incremental growth by simply just focusing on winning the day. I implore you to expect the best out of yourself. We can all rest well at night knowing we checked off several things that were accomplished in the day, which in turn will lead to a positive upward trend. For example, if your desire is to get in better physical shape, you can walk one more step than you did the prior day. How about improving your mental shape? You can read one more sentence than you did the day prior. What about growing spiritually? You can read one more chapter than the prior day. When you do the calculation on this, it would equate to significant growth day by day. I am not saying you should aspire for this amount of growth daily, but you can at the very least attain one percent improvement each day.

The first victory we can all have each day is against that good ole opportunity clock and rising before the sun. If you do not use an alarm, I would suggest winning the battle of hitting your knees first thing over checking your phone. I would bet the majority of you reading this do not have this issue, but according to studies, this is not the case for majority of people. According to a survey [9] from Reviews.org, 89 percent of people check their phone within the first ten minutes of waking up and check their phones an average of 144 times per day. The survey found that, on average, Americans spend two hours, fifty-four minutes on their phones each day. That means that the average American will spend nearly a month and a half (forty-four days) on their phones in a single year. I would bet that if you look at the usage on your device, you would be surprised at what you find.

These were just a few of the several statistics from the survey of one thousand Americans eighteen and older regarding their cell phone usage and habits. This shows that most people cannot be without their phone without feeling uneasy. The things we treasure typically will be in close proximity to us at all times. This study also found that 45 percent of Americans call it their most valuable possession. When I first came across this study, it reminded me of Matthew 6:21: "For where your treasure is, there will your heart be also." We must take inventory of the treasure we all have and identify what truly has our heart while being intentional with who we give it to. The majority of the world is obsessed with things that are corrupt, and if we are to be wise, we can avoid being like most. I think it's best to follow the advice outlined in Matthew 6:19–20: "Lay not up for yourselves treasures upon earth, where moth and rust doth corrupt, and where thieves break through and steal; but lay up for yourselves treasures in heaven, where neither moth nor rust doth corrupt, and where thieves do not break through nor steal." You might not need a reminder of this, but in case you do, the thief cometh not, but for to steal, and to kill, and to destroy. It is your decision if you allow this to happen. Every day you have an opportunity to fill your cup and avoid it from being stolen.

Questions to ask yourself as it pertains to personal growth

1. **Am I investing enough in myself?** Nothing is more important as a leader than personal daily growth.
2. **What is not serving me purposefully?** Let go of anything preventing you from growing.
3. **Do I have goals for personal growth?** If not, why not?
4. **Am I genuinely investing in others?** Your motives matter. There is a big difference between people who are genuinely wanting to help others and those who are in it for themselves.
5. **Am I adding value to those in my circle?** The more value you add to your circle, you increase the chances of getting more back in return.
6. **Did I make today count?** Govern the clock; don't be governed by it!
7. **Am I investing in the right people?** The wrong people will be a waste of time!

You will drink out of several "cups" in your life. It will start will a sippy cup and end with your favorite cup of choice. I challenge you to keep a perspective of what you are doing with yours at all times. Pay attention to your input, and take heed to the advice given in 1 Corinthians 11:28: "But let a man examine himself, and so let him eat of that bread, and drink of that cup." Might I add that Solomon, the man full of wisdom, said in Proverbs 11:25, "The liberal soul shall be made fat: and he that watereth shall be watered also himself." So, no matter the cup you hold, make sure it's not empty!

Challenge #14 I challenge you follow a personal growth plan and pour into yourself each day. *I would love to hear about the growth plan you follow and the ways you fill up your cup. If you are willing to share, please use the hashtag #YCDI.*

Chapter Fifteen
IT'S AN INSIDE JOB

In the early parts of 2017, I went on a quest to discover the things preventing me from achieving the next level of success in my business. Little did I know, I would find more than what I was initially looking for. This time in my life was what most would consider a rough patch. The hurdles on the professional side of business were nothing in comparison to things I had to overcome in my personal life. The reward in all of this is that I would learn more about myself this year compared to any year prior. That following year in April, I was on trajectory to achieve over 50 percent + growth in sales by year end (finished with 52.9 percent growth), which led to me being asked to share some of the things I learned and executed within my business to have exponential growth.

The individuals in attendance were a group of top executives and owners from a Fortune 500 company. The location was in beautiful Nassau, Bahamas, at the Grand Hyatt Baha Mar. This is one of my favorite places to vacation, so of course I could not pass up on this opportunity. When I got the call to speak, it was in the middle of taking care of excrement and disposing dung. The individual who called asked if I was busy, and I said, "Not really. Just doing a good ole number two." At this time in my life, I got really serious about having every hour of each day accounted for, but I never made time for this activity, so if I got an important call during this special time of day, I would always answer it no matter what and would always be honest if someone asked, "Are you busy?"

I believe it is best to be honest at all times, and I realize I was probably too honest at this point. I tell you this story because it was during this call, I came up with what I call the "shit ratio," and I felt compelled to share the understanding with the group. I came to the realization that just like every man and woman who must partake in this same daily activity all of our days, we must also overcome our fair share of it daily. This then caused me to stop and think about the number of unfortunate events or problems that had to be solved in my business during any given week in comparison to the number of people I would was responsible to lead. By doing this, I was able to develop this understanding that gave me a sense of peace as I encountered problems and additions to the team.

The flight I took to arrive at the destination experienced turbulence, and this gave me inspiration to add this as a talking point. During that speech, it is safe to say I did not hold back, and the response I received was overwhelming. The group consisted primarily of business owners, and the majority (51 percent) were below double-digit growth or were in the negative (36 percent). The standard for the company was nothing less than ten percent growth year over year. The first thing I reminded the group of was that they were all proven champions. They would not have been in that room if it were not the case. I had to remind them of this and make sure they all believed this, so I asked them all to raise their hand if they still had this belief about themselves, and the entire room raised their hands. This signified that I was given permission to not only speak to them but address them as such. I went on to share with them that I did not have it all figured out. I still to this day have so many areas to improve in and get better at. But I learned growth starts when you are able to look in the mirror and not point the finger out the window.

Speaking engagement 2018 SGA Meeting

It was very humbling to be speaking to a room full of millionaires and accomplished individuals on the subject of growth for the third consecutive time after having consecutive years in the red. I told them, "So I am supposed to talk about GROWTH, but did you know in 2016 and 2017 I did not have growth? I am living proof you can turn your business around. Today, my goal is to leave you all with action items to help those who are serious about their growth and willing to execute. What I would like to share today is FIVE STEPS TO GROWTH that anyone here can follow. But before I go into these things, I need you all to understand nothing I have done is extraordinary or outside of the landscape of normal business practice. But the key for me was finally getting serious about growing myself. I must first start by giving glory to God, my support system, accountability partners, and my team."

It is a must to give credit where it is due because when these things are missing, even when someone decides to go after internal growth, it will be more challenging to grow your business without these factors. Here are the following steps that were discussed, and you can also use them at any time to have growth in any area your life:

Step 1: TAKE INVENTORY OF YOUR PERSONAL GROWTH PLAN (PGP)

Take time to identify how much time you invest in yourself versus others. What I found out when doing this for the first time was that my ratio was off, and this led made me to make an adjustment to my personal growth plan. This confirmed to me that this process will always be greater than results. Around this same time Marcus asked me a priceless question: "What is the most important thing to you between taking care of your spirit, mind, or body?" His goal was to help me uncover how to prioritize things based on what is important to me. This question led to me learning that it is an inside job! Effective leadership starts on the inside, and sometimes we must realign things. We have to align our head, heart, hands, and habits to that of growth. Just how we tune up our vehicles every so often to ensure it will run properly, the same rule applies to us all individually.

Step 2: COMMIT TO YOUR PGP

You know when someone is on the right path of commitment when they visit the accountability mirror often. This is a very important step to commitment as I learned self-deception is like the fog that covers the mirror after taking a steamy shower. When things get steamy, beware of self-deception; it will prevent you from seeing things as they are. It is best to clear the fog and embrace a few moments of brutal honesty regarding your commitment as it will save you years of self-deception. No matter the occasion, it will always be best to pay the price of commitment.

Step 3: SERVE

When you are on the journey of growth, it is obvious you must pour into yourself, but the main ingredient is that you must then pour into others. The more people you serve, the more you will be served. You do not have to be great to serve, but you have to serve to be great. How you serve is more important than what you serve. Lastly, serve something bigger than yourself. It states in Matthew 6:24: "No man can serve two masters: for either he will hate the one and love the other; or else he will hold to the one and despise the other. Ye cannot serve God and mammon." A great reminder on being sure of what you choose to serve. As for me and my house, we will serve the Lord.

Step 4: PARTNER UP

When you find a trusted accountability partner, they will be your truth-teller and will help you avoid self-deception. This trusted individual will also help in the inspection process your PGP. All wise men who follow the advice given in Proverbs 15:22 have a higher chance of victory: "Without counsel purposes are disappointed: but in the multitude of counsellors, they are established". It also says in Proverbs 11:14: "Where no counsel is, the people fall: but in the multitude of counselors there is safety."

Step 5: NO EGO

When you think of ego, what is the first thing that comes to mind? Typically, we think of something that is self-centered. We all have suffered from this battle at some point in our lives, and those who are honest about it are able to overcome this hurdle. I have come to learn that when I am operating from an ego perspective, I am essentially **Edging God Out.** Regardless of your beliefs, I would highly recommend you to not try and control things out of your control; instead, get in the passenger seat and enjoy the ride by **Exalting God Only.** He who humbles himself will be exalted, and he who exalts himself will be humbled. I have found it best to exalt him instead. Growing up in Ohio, we learned the state motto at an early age: "With God, all things are possible." And when I first learned of this, it was my first exposure on ego. My Lord and Saviour made reference of this very important reminder, which has helped me get through my own ego battles.

This inside job journey led me on a search within the innermost parts of my temple to light a candle. I told the group about this outcome and defined it as inner research in the darkness. Since then, I have continued on the journey to let that light shine and keep it on a candlestick amongst the darkness in the world. When you fall in love with wisdom, that light will never go out. You have probably heard the saying, "Early to bed, early to rise keeps one healthy, wealthy, and wise." I implore you to rise early and be committed and submitted to becoming the best version of yourself in all your endeavors as you will light your own candle. Never go a moment in your life without a "PGP," and understand you must pay the price without negotiating. Just like we must exercise the muscles to avoid atrophy, it is imperative to exercise your mind and spirit to avoid atrophy. I want to give a special shout-out to all the individuals over the years who were a part of my journey of self-development avoiding atrophy and all the individuals teams I lead which now get the glory. Let this be your reminder that no man can build something worth talking about by himself.

Challenge #15 I challenge you search the innermost parts of your temple. *I would love to hear about the ways you do so. If you are willing to share, please use the hashtag #YCDI.*

Chapter Sixteen
LOVE

The word *love* appears over six hundred times in the Bible, and in the original Hebrew tongue it is pronounced *Ahab*. It is also worth noting the word is mentioned almost three times more than hate. Love is more than just a word, and everyone in tune with the feeling will agree they cannot go without it. Even water is influenced by it and responds to the impact of feeling love. There was an experiment done using rice by Dr. Masaru Emoto, who proved this point to be true. He discovered that human thoughts and intentions can alter physical reality, in his rice experiment it was the molecular structure of water. He was able to show that water changes by the way you interact with it. Positive or negative. It feels you; it is aware of you. Why is this important to know? The human body is made of majority water. What I learned about the experiment is that what goes on inside the body is largely affected by external things, but most importantly we should be aware of the power of our actions and words.

When it comes to this subject, there is not one person I met who truly has no desire to be loved. Now the way we go about speaking to each other's love language is complicated, to say the least. I have always responded best to quality time and physical touch. I am sure this stems from my childhood. I can recall the many times I was sick as a kid and would lay my head on my mother's lap. The moment she rubbed my head it was like all sickness disappeared. She also worked long hours and did not have the luxury to be a stay-at-home mom, which made it hard to get my idea of desired quantity time with her. But the time we spent together felt more quality than anything. Now I will take quality over quantity anytime, but it never hurt anyone to have a good mixture of the two. Do you know your love language? The better question is, have you shared it with those you love? The best question, especially for those married, is are you speaking your spouse's love language? It is necessary to understand the love language of the individuals with whom you invest the most time. Well, that is only if you desire to avoid the complication of not knowing so.

Love language can be found in many environments if you look for it. When you decide not to bring love into the environments you enter, do not expect to receive or find it. Love should be a part of everyone's lifestyle, which can be expressed in so many different ways. For example, the time you dedicate to your children is an expression of how much you value and love them. They might not remember all the time you spend with them, but they will for sure remember the time when you did not for a lifetime. People who love themselves also have discipline. You can look at the physical appearance of someone and their level of discipline will tell you whether they love themselves. Love and discipline will always mate well without any complications.

There is a force that pushes us all to transcend, and it is love. The will to extend your spiritual growth revolves around love. When you love your spirit, you will work daily to keep the lamp lit. When you love your body, you will take care of it by watching what you consume. When you love you mind, you will make sure to put the right things in and protect it at all costs. All of these things are expressions of self-love, which leads to growth. When we grow it is because we are working at it, and we are working at it because we love ourselves. It is through love that we elevate ourselves and through our love for others we help others elevate themselves.

Loving people are growing people. If we want to be loved, we must make ourselves lovable. When you truly love someone, you will make an intentional effort to show them. Regardless of others picking up on this action, it is always best to put out love. There are no excuses when it comes to this; you either do it or you do not, and it is all shown by our actions. Do not make the mistake of trying to use the excuse of many by telling yourself you do not know how to love others. I admit I said this to myself a few times before while looking in the mirror and acknowledging it was an excuse. I was not only making an excuse, but this prevented me from experiencing more of the effects of loving on others. My justification was that growing up I did not "feel loved," but with identifying how much this hurt myself and others, I was forced to change my perspective. I have since been able to bury this stronghold through learning about the different ways to love others, but more importantly how to properly love myself. If we are supposed to love our neighbor like we love ourselves, the only problem I see with this is when we do not know how to love ourselves.

Love should be present in the professional arena as well. When you are not operating in the realm of what you love doing, it will feel like work. But when you do what you love it becomes a hobby. I suggest finding what you love doing, and usually it will revolve around something you are really good at. Yes, you have to start at the amateur level, but if you keep at your craft and pay the price by putting in 10,000 hours, you will eventually become an elite professional. We all have choices, and with those choices we can choose to do what we love. I love seeking wisdom and understanding. I love being a husband and father. I love becoming the best version of myself. I love serving people and helping others become the best version of themselves. Teaching its part of my calling. I love coaching people and helping them achieve their goals. I can honestly say it is one of the few things that has come close to how I feel when doing inner research and discovering truth. I implore you to find what you love doing. I have found that if you fill your entire day with productive things you are good at, the outcome is you will love what you do.

When it comes to leadership, I learned you must love people before trying to lead them. We have all heard the saying, "People don't care how much you know until they know how much you care." Well, try that with love; it is the same way. People don't care to love you until they know you love them. True servant leaders get people to follow them because of love not fear. They love people before trying to lead them. I believe the obstacles of love would be easy to overcome if we all followed the instructions about the royal law written in James 2:8 says, "If ye fulfil the royal law according to the scripture, Thou shalt love thy neighbour as thyself, ye do well." Not all neighbors will be the same, and some will be harder to love than others. But if you look for the good in everyone, you can find something. This might require exercise of patience to find it, but we all possess qualities that enable love.

Did you know that if you put one hundred black ants and one hundred red ants in a jar, nothing will happen? But if you shake the jar hard, the ants will start killing each other. The red ants consider the black ants their enemy while the black ants consider the red ants their enemy also. The same is true for us in the world. The true enemy is the one shaking the jar. This happens in our society each and every day. So, before we attack each other, we should think about who is shaking the jar in this battle we call life. Consider what Paul wrote to the Ephesians to understand the real battle we are all up against. "Put on the whole armour of God, that ye may be able to stand against the wiles of the devil. For we wrestle not against flesh and blood, but against principalities, against powers, against the rulers of the darkness of this world, against spiritual wickedness in high places. Wherefore take unto you the whole armour of God, that ye may be able to withstand in the evil day, and having done all, to stand. Stand therefore, having your loins girt about with truth, and having on the breastplate of righteousness; And your feet shod with the preparation of the gospel of peace; Above all, taking the shield of faith, wherewith ye shall be able to quench all the fiery darts of the wicked. And take the helmet of salvation, and the sword of the Spirit, which is the word of God" (Ephesians 6:11–17). In simple terms, if you stay ready you do not have to get ready.

Loving our neighbor is not the finish line as we are reminded of this in Deuteronomy 6:5: "And thou shalt love the Lord thy God with all thine heart, and with all thy soul, and with all thy might." Let work together to change the narrative and not be like most people who will do more to keep intact their friendship with people but will not do the same thing with God. Yes, it is okay to have respect of your relationship with people, but this should not take precedence over the relationship you have with God. It is worth nothing that with friends come accountability, and someone who cares about you will not let this happen. In 2 Timothy 3:1–8 we are given a friendly reminder of the type of person we all will become if we concentrate on putting our love into the wrong thing: "This know also, that in the last days perilous times shall come. For men shall be lovers of their own selves, covetous, boasters, proud, blasphemers, disobedient to parents, unthankful, unholy, without natural affection, trucebreakers, false accusers, incontinent, fierce, despisers of those that are good, traitors, heady, high-minded, lovers of pleasures more than lovers of God; having a form of godliness, but denying the power thereof: from such turn away. For of this sort are they which creep into houses, and lead captive silly women laden with sins, led away with divers lusts, ever learning, and never able to come to the knowledge of the truth. Now as Jannes and Jambres withstood Moses, so do these also resist the truth: men of corrupt minds, reprobate concerning the faith."

Let's all avoid being in this category when these days come. Some would argue we are living in the last days, and I would not disagree, but who really knows. It reads in Matthew 24: 36–37: "But of that day and hour knoweth no man, no, not the angels of heaven, but my Father only. But as the days on Noe were, so shall also the coming of the Son of man be." We are told in Matthew 25:13 to "watch therefore, for ye know neither the day nor the hour wherein the Son of man cometh." Truth be told no one actually knows the time, but we do have signs to look out for, and if you are paying attention things do correlate. Regardless of what is going on around us, we can all live in such a way where we strive to love and serve. There is a reward for serving also: "Blessed is that servant, whom his lord when he cometh shall find so doing" (Matthew 24:46).

Five simple rules on love I choose to live by:

1. Love yourself first.
2. Love those closest to you.
3. Love the process.
4. Love what matters most.
5. Do what you love to do.

One of my favorite verses on love can be found in Joshua 22:5: "But take diligent heed to do the commandment and the law, which Moses the servant of the LORD charged you, to love the LORD your God, and to walk in all his ways, and to keep his commandments, and to cleave unto him, and to serve him with all your heart and with all your soul." This hits deeper when coupled with 1 John 5:3: "For this is the love of God, that we keep his commandments: and his commandments are not grievous." I encourage you all to love your neighbor as yourself. Hopefully, you have found what you enjoy doing and dedicating yourself to the work. Let us not forget if you ever want to defeat hatred respond with LOVE!

Challenge #16 I challenge you to love yourself first and then spread that love to others. Play your role in putting out positivity into the world. Here is a question you should ask yourself often: Do you love who you are becoming? Whether the answer is yes or no, I want to memorialize that the person who has the key to unlock the answer you desire will always be yourself. *I would love to hear about it. If you are willing to share, please use the hashtag #YCDI.*

Chapter Seventeen

WHAT DO YOU WANT YOUR DASH TO REPRESENT?

The day you were born and the day your soul leaves this place will be two different journeys. One we get to choose as our final destination; the other was thankfully chosen for us as a gift. Now what we do with that gift is how we show appreciation to the One who formed us in the womb. Another way of looking at this is realizing that every person born will have two days associated with their name. What I have found is that the dash is seldom talked about much around dinner tables. Now I am not talking about a race on the track, which is often referred to as a dash. I am talking about the dash on the tombstone.

You will hear topics of all kinds at tables across the world, and rightfully so. But I bet most of you reading this have yet to embark much on this topic at the table you were raised. Why am I so confident in this? Well, according to data from the company Statista [10], just 11 percent of us consider the subject of death in our daily lives. Most of us are clearly "busy" with the subject of life, perhaps only considering the subject three or four times a year. It usually occurs during the not-so-fun discussions, such as when we have a loved one pass on. That dash in the middle is like having a layover. If you have never experienced a layover, it can be good or bad; it is all relative to the perspective of the individual and how they choose to manage the event. I have done my fair share of traveling around various airports, and if you observe the individuals waiting for their flight, you can find them doing everything from enjoying the lounge facilities, sleeping, buying unnecessary materialistic items, eating, being merry, conversing, reading, and rushing,—just to name a few. People approach their life the same way and seldom forget that the plane to your "final destination" will take off whether you are ready or not. Have you ever considered what gate will you walk through? What flight will you be taking out of here? Have you booked your final destination? If you have, where to?

I know these are tough questions to ponder upon, but it is best to consider a thoughtful moment of uncomfortability than to spend eternity in regret wondering. Life is pretty much the same way as the layover as we are passing by for a short period of time. During this time, you will seldom be faced with some kind of test, but your perspective will play a role in your outcome. I must admit most layover flights I have taken definitely tested my patience. Whether you like it or not, I can guarantee throughout the course of life you will be faced with your fair share of tests. I encourage you to pass each test and stay ready for the flight. There will come a time when that final destination is ready for each passenger who is assigned a seat to see the One who formed you in the womb.

The price we must all pay for that ticket starts with faith and ends with submission while following instructions. Now whether you strive to personally know the Teacher responsible for the test and forming you or not is your prerogative, but I believe we should all be thankful we have a Teacher who believe in us all and would like to see us all ace the test. We can even rely on him as he is our hope and strength as it states in Joel 3:16. Over time, we all will come to realize that at some point what happens during the dash is about endurance and repentance. It is best to run your race and repent for not doing the right things during your dash before you talk with the Teacher.

By the way, it is cool to repent of your sins and be baptized if you desire to see the kingdom. As it says in John 3:3–5, "Jesus answered and said unto him, Verily, verily, I say unto thee, Except a man be born again, he cannot see the kingdom of God. Nicodemus saith unto him, How can a man be born when he is old? can he enter the second time into his mother's womb, and be born? Jesus answered, Verily, verily, I say unto thee, Except a man be born of water and of the Spirit, he cannot enter into the kingdom of God."

My advice is to kill that old man and do not allow the things of the world to get in the way of you doing either. Here is the best thing about doing them both: as you run your race you do not have to be a marathon runner to endure. It is totally fine to sprint toward your purpose in life and rely on wisdom (*Ruwach* in Hebrew, see *Strong's* H7307). As you approach each day you hopefully wake up with an attitude of gratitude for being afforded more time to do something productive with your dash.

One of my favorite scriptures about running can be found in 1 Corinthians 9:24: "Know ye not that they which run in a race run all, but one receiveth the prize? So run, that ye may obtain." The prize for winning the race is worth it, and it will not collect dust unlike the trophies and medals that are rewarded on earth to the top runners. There is no limit on the amount crowns to be rewarded. In this race, we all have an opportunity at the grand prize. For anyone who has ever ran track competitively, you know it is best to stay in your lane and never be worried about anyone else in the other lanes. Why? Because fortunately we can only control what we do in the race.

Be thankful you can control the outcome of your dash as we all know someone who never had that opportunity. If you are like me, you look forward to one day seeing the seed of yours who were formed in the womb with a heartbeat but never had the chance at either dash. On April 10, 2022, I experienced what this felt like with the loss of Tahlia James Cunningham. This was by far one of the hardest days my wife, daughter, and I had to endure. Although it was a very challenging time, it also brought our family closer, and we were able to find out who we could lean on during that difficult time. I still have challenges of controlling my emotions whenever I have thoughts about my dear daughter, who I had to bury at just twenty-one weeks. Just the thought of seeing her beautiful face again brings me to tears, but I am also comforted in knowing one day I will see her again. Each time I visit her tombstone or see morning dew, I am reminded of her and this very thing we call life that is often taken for granted. I have attended several funerals, but I never thought growing up I would have to pick out a casket and tombstone for my own child. I share this to remind you to not take life for granted.

You all have heard the saying, "The graveyard is full of dreams unfulfilled," but I would bet that the majority of these same individuals, if given the chance to do their dash all over again, they would. The problem here is this is not how life works as we only get one shot at life. My advice for you is to exhaust everything you have within your DNA while you have time. Live your life on purpose with no regrets, and do not be like the individuals who wish they had a second chance to do it all over again.

April 4, 1984, was the day I was finished being formed in the womb and made my entrance into the world. I do not know the date or time for my destination flight, but I told myself before the age of accountability that I will make sure to make the most of my dash with the temporary time afforded. I encourage you to avoid being too busy and to do the same with the time you have remaining. Take accountability for everything you do in life now while you have time, and make sure everything you do is relative to your desired final stop. It is easy to forget, but let me remind you we were all given a temporary life to prove you deserve a permanent one. Pay the price it costs for the permanent life you desire to have while you still have time. Do not be a fool and waste your talents away. One day, every heart will stop beating and we will have to give an account for all the things we did while living. How do you want that conversation to go? I aspire to hear, "Well done, good and faithful servant." I aspire to sow seeds into good ground and bring forth fruit while helping those that are lost in life find their way.

No matter what you face at this present moment in life, your story matters. I encourage you to tell your story and yes, we all have a "sad one" to tell. You will either use yours as motivation or as an excuse. My advice to you is to let your trials, tribulations, successes, and failures be someone else's survival guide. Never be afraid to shine your light. I want you to know if we do not do what we are called to do in this game of life, we are of no use to the world. If you know why you play the game, even if your time is up before anticipated, you shall win. But if you forget why you are playing, then even if you win you lose.

Lastly, you cannot lose if you do not quit. I would also like to add that who you are is more important than what you do. In knowing this, we can avoid the typical pitfall of many, which is becoming so busy with life you forget about your purpose. Imagine hearing you wasted your entire life doing everything but that which you were called to do. This conversation has to be up there with one of the worst to ever take place. We will all find out one day as no man or woman can dodge the sentencing when we arrive to meet the plaintiff and hear all of our contributions and charges. I encourage you to use your time wisely so when that conversation ends, your name is in the Book of Life.

Challenge #17 I challenge you to carefully think about what you want your dash to represent. Regardless if you have never thought about it, I want to memorialize that the person who has the key to unlock all that you desire will always be the same person who stares directly at you whenever you look in the mirror. *I would love to hear about what you want your dash to represent. If you are willing to share, please use the hashtag #YCDI.*

CONCLUSION

In conclusion, as we reach the end of this journey, I want to leave you with this powerful truth: you are capable of achieving greatness. It is important to realize your potential is often marked by challenges and obstacles. However, it is precisely in these moments of adversity that the belief in oneself becomes most crucial. I encourage you to reflect on the stories and lessons shared in the book, and to draw inspiration from individuals who have defied the odds and achieved remarkable feats through unwavering self-belief. Throughout these pages, we have explored the depths of human potential and witnessed the transformative power of belief. The belief in oneself is not just a passive state of mind, but an active force that drives action and perseverance, and the spark that ignites extraordinary achievements. Cultivate a resilient mindset, embrace failure as a stepping-stone to success, and consistently challenge your own perceived limitations. By doing so you can tap into your inner reservoir of strength and determination and propel yourself towards your aspirations.

Finally, your belief not only impacts your own life, but also has the potential to inspire those around you. Yes, you have the potential to inspire and uplift those around you. Share your journey, struggles, and triumphs with others I promise you it is a pure source of encouragement and empowerment for those who may be struggling to believe in their own potential. Now it is time for you to embrace your own potential and believe in your ability to overcome challenges, pursue your dreams, and make a meaningful impact.

As you close this book, carry with you the unwavering conviction that YOU CAN DO IT! Let that belief propel you toward a future filled with endless possibilities. Ignore what they tell you. Use your "unfortunate" life circumstances to your advantage. Do not ever let anyone tell you that you cannot do something. Instead, always tell yourself YOU CAN DO IT!

BIBLIOGRAPHY

1. Finkelhor, D., Hotaling, G., Lewis, I. A., & Smith, C. (1990). Sexual abuse in a national survey of adult men and women: Prevalence, characteristics, and risk factors. Child Abuse & Neglect 14, 19-28. doi:10.1016/0145-2134(90)90077-7
2. Dinkes R, Cataldi EF, Lin-Kelly W. *Indicators of School Crime and Safety: 2007 (NCES 2008-021/NCJ 219553)* Washington, D.C.: Institute of Education Sciences, U.S. Department of Education, and Bureau of Justice Statistics, Office of Justice Programs, U.S. Department of Justice; 2007.
3. Kottusch P, Tillmann M, Püschel K. Oberlebenszeit bei Nahrungs- und Flüssigkeitskarenz [Survival time without food and drink]. Arch Kriminol. 2009 Nov-Dec;224(5-6):184-91. German. PMID: 20069776.
4. https://www.ncaa.org/sports/2013/12/17/probability-of-competing-beyond-high-school.aspx
5. Reardon CL, et al. Br J Sports Med 2019;53:667–699. doi:10.1136/bjsports-2019-100715
6. https://archive.blogs.harvard.edu/abinazir/2011/06/15/what-are-chances-you-would-be-born/
7. https://www.pbsnc.org/blogs/science/how-many-decisions-do-we-make-in-one-day/
8. http://poncefoundation.com/christians-dont-read-their-bible/
9. https://www.reviews.org/mobile/cell-phone-addiction/
10. https://www.sciencefocus.com/the-human-body/are-we-thinking-about-death-wrong

ACKNOWLEDGMENTS

This book was years in the making, and many hours were spent walking on the treadmill writing at my gym, in my home office, and at my local coffee house putting this together. Given the opportunity to write this book was a gift, and I had to decide how to use that gift. My deepest gratitude goes to my virtuous rib for working with me throughout this journey to ensure that I pass this gift along to you.

Marissa (babe), you made it very easy for me to write this book. Only you know how hard this process was for me to complete. It was years in the making. Your unwavering support and continual sacrifice over the years have been priceless. You have been by my side through majority of the ups and downs. Together, we have endured many trials, tribulations, and hoped for things only God knows. We have built a life together that I would not trade for anything. It is because of you I was able to put the time in to accomplish this goal of mine, and not once did you give me a hard time. For this I truly appreciate you. You have been the helpmeet I always desired, and you truly make it so that I can do so many things with ease. All I can say is thank you and I love you.

To my daughter, Cianna, you are so smart, beautiful, strong, and fearfully and wonderfully made. You have been blessed with many gifts, and it brings me pure joy to see you use those gifts. I want you to know I will always be by your side and protect you as long as my heart beats. In your own special way, you give me hope. You also bring joy to Mom and me. I appreciate you checking in with me on the progress of the book during our car rides to school, knowing it took longer than anticipated to finish. You challenged me to complete this in a timely manner and to not put it off. I look forward to reading your book one day and witnessing you inspire others. I love you and am proud to be your dad.

There are so many people to thank, but I want to acknowledge the following individuals as you all helped make this possible. I would not be the person I am without your impact on my life:

My sister Dorothy. Our lives and the way we grew up were not easy. You always kept me on my toes and drove me crazy at times, but one thing I can say is that you were always there for me when I needed you. I appreciate you very much. I will always be your big brother, although I am the middle.

My sister Jamelia, I tried my best to protect you growing up, and although I was overprotective, I can assure you it was because I love you and wanted nothing but the best for you. We have had a lot of disagreements over time, and I want to you to know this never affected my love for you.

Troy, I look forward to the day when you read the chapter dedicated to you and hearing from you. I sincerely want you to know how much those words inspired me throughout my life. I have never been the same, and for that I thank you.

Fred and Sheila Kressierer, I am not sure where my life would be if we would have never crossed paths. One thing is for certain: God makes no mistakes, and there is a reason we crossed paths. I promise to always live up to the promise I made to you. There is no way I could ever pay you back for what you did for me. I am forever grateful to you.

Diane Zellmer, I want to give you flowers. I am confident there are not many people in the world with a heart the size of yours. You have cared for so many people in their worst times, too many to count. I am one of those individuals, and there is no way I could ever pay you back for all the things you have done in my life. I appreciate you from the bottom of my heart.

Rebecca Doak, you gave me hope at a time in my life when I did not know what I would do with myself. You have made a major impact on my life, and I am certain if you would not have accepted the meeting with me, my life would not be the same. I am thankful you were at Mount Union when I attended and thank you for being a servant.

Nick Zangardi, you are responsible for so many lives being changed, mine being one of them. You are a legend in the financial services industry, and I will never forget what you did for me. I remember the challenges I had to overcome at the beginning of my career, and you never turned your back. Thank you for believing in me, training me, guiding me, and listening to Marcus to recruit at our alma mater. Love you, Z Unit.

James Surace, as I said earlier in the book, I could write a novel on how great of a man you are in my eyes. You truly were the first example of good man, and the way you have lived is inspiring to so many people, including myself. I thank you for planting the seed in me and investing in me to grow in my relationship with the Lord. JS, thank you from the bottom of my heart. I love you!

Marcus Smith, "Weezy," you are hands-down one of the baddest to ever do it. Many, including myself, did not understand how great of a leader you are while under your tutelage. As I have gotten closer to you, it is hard to put into words how much you mean to me. Yes, I was a knucklehead and rough around the edges, but it is because of you I truly learned how to transform myself from the inside. Thank you for making us all dogs and pushing us to become great. I am forever thankful to you!

Steve Surace, there has never been a better trainer in the history of the company. I am so thankful you were present for my training. Had it been someone else, I am confident I would not have continued. Thank you for being a real one and helping me through every phase of my career.

Simon Arias, I owe you a sincere amount of gratitude for taking me under your wings in the beginning to being by my side through each phase of my career. You are the big brother I always wanted. I know for certain if you were not around in the beginning stages, it would have been very difficult to endure. Thank you for your being a real one. And yes, you are one of the baddest to ever do it.

Jamison Weatherspoon, my brother from another, I have so much to say about you and the man, father, husband, and leader you are. You are very special, and I can say had you not taken the leap of faith to join me, life would not be the same. I am forever thankful for you and appreciate all you have done in my life.

Michael Vasu, my friend, you played a role in my career early on that I could never repay you for. You invested in me when you did not have to, from the time you showed me how to do things to the first book I ever received on leadership. Oh yeah, I also remember the video recorder you gifted me. The talk we had outside was a defining moment in my career, and I know for certain you positively influenced me in a way no one else could have. Mike, thank you for being a real one and caring about me when you did not have to.

Patrick "Bulldog" Bendure, from the Screwy Lewy days to the beginning of my career, you were always one that inspired me. I thank you for always checking in on me and challenging me in ways that helped me grow as a leader.

Alex Grakhov, "Rocket," although you almost killed us during my field training, I am thankful you were the one responsible for showing me how to make it happen. I learned some valuable things from you and thank you for being patient with me.

John Ophals, you took a leap of faith and moved to Indiana with us to start the organization from scratch. And although you were a knucklehead like I was, I appreciate all you did to ensure that we would successfully grow. Your loyalty has never gone unnoticed, and you will forever hold a special place in my heart.

IP Harris, we came up in the business together and went through a lot along the way. I am happy to see you become a husband and father to a beautiful family. I promise you if you did not marry Jess, I would have strangled you. All joking aside, I thank you for all the sacrifices you made over the years and the impact you made to help build the foundation. We would not have laid the foundation the way we did if you would not have taken a leap of faith.

Emily Heron, you were the best assistant I could have ever had. I tell Marissa there is no other woman who could put up with me. But as I wrote this book, I come to realize you are part of the select few. You truly were my ride or die, and I would not have been able to function without you being a major pillar to the organization. I am happy to see the woman you have become and the family you and Kyle have built. You are a first-class individual, and I appreciate everything you did not only for me but the entire organization over the decade-plus of our time together. Love you!

Roger Smith, I appreciate you being a one of one type of CEO. I am thankful you were at the helm when I came into the company. I will never forget the workout we had and the time we spent together when I was first promoted. From day one, your story inspired and gave me hope to know anything was possible. Thank you for your leadership and your belief in me.

Scott ("The Man") Smith, you are the reason I was promoted, and I thank you for making sure we were taken care of during that transition. You rolled your sleeves up and helped me grow into a businessman. Thank you for opening your house to me and being a phone call away throughout the duration of my career.

Richard Meshulam, you taught me the importance of doing business with quality. I do not take for granted the time you invested in me over all the years. I remember the visit you made to Indiana and how you reminded me before you left that someone would be Judas. You were right! And despite having to endure these scenarios over the years, it was all worth it. PS: Your dry humor was top notch and will never be defeated.

Bernard Rappaport, I remember shaking your hand at my first owners meeting. I was shy to hold a conversation with you, but I remember you telling me I would do great things with the company, and you'd heard great things about me. Still after all these years, I think of you every month, and we all are forever indebted to you for creating the amazing company.

Scott Niedzwiecki, thank you for showing me what true coaching is all about. You made an impact on my life more than you can imagine. I will never forget the walk we took and the wisdom you poured into me. I still wish we would have won it all for you as you deserved it, but nevertheless, we accomplished some great things together. By the way, I can still kick your butt in a game of basketball. Love you coach!

John Gibbons, I remember sitting with you in the cafeteria reviewing your notes as you prepared for our rival game. You are a man of many talents and could have given Bob Knight a run for his money with throwing chairs. Although some misunderstood your style of coaching, I always enjoyed playing for you. Congrats on your retirement and induction. You earned it.

Michael Bailey, you were the first coach who truly believed in me. Thank you for investing into me and treating me like a son. I remember the drives and shoes you purchased for me when I could not afford them. I also remember you busting one while doing a demonstration on the long jump pit in your dress shoes. That moment will never go away. And trust me, I have had my fair share of bloopers. You were the coolest coach I ever ran for. I adopted a lot of your coaching styles and hope to have as much of an impact on my athletes like you had for those who ran for you. Congratulations on your retirement and induction. It is well-deserved.

John Homon, you are a legend in track and field. I can write a book on the infamous things you said to me. I think of you often as I tell my "athletes on the whistle." You were the most unique coach I ever had and the only one who knew how to really push me. You made me do things I did not want to do. It took me some years to understand the importance and power of embracing things you dislike, but I got it. I now embrace those things and I have to give you credit as you were instrumental to my foundation of proving people wrong in life. Congratulations on being inducted into the hall of fame. Love you, Coach!

Larry Kehres, there is no doubt you are the best football coach I ever played for. There is a reason you have the highest winning percentage in college football history. It is a testament to the way you developed us all into men. I am happy to have played for you and to have learned valuable lessons from you. You are the only man I have ever allowed to put saliva on the palms of my hands. At the time, I thought it was the most odd thing ever, but over time I understood the lesson you taught me. I have kept my promise and will continue to do good in life.

Jordan Burns, the best chiropractor in the world. You are more than a chiropractor. I would not be the same without the work you have done on me. I also want to thank you for helping guide me through this process of writing my book. It would have taken a lot longer to complete. Thank you, brother!

Elder Rawchaashayar and Elder Lawya, double honors to you both for your unwavering commitment to the work you both have done. I am forever grateful to have found you two. I no longer walk in ignorance, and I sincerely thank you both for teaching me the doctrine the way it was intended. All the lessons have given me an understanding that cannot be measured. Like you say, all the time I plan to finish and play my part. Thank you for showing me true purpose in life.

Deacon Gabar Yahalah, thank you for helping me get baptized in the true name of the Father, Son, and Holy Spirit. I appreciate your hospitality and the love you have displayed for me and my family since day one. I love you like a big brother and thank you for being patient with me on this walk. You are someone I know I can lean on to give me true guidance, and I do not take for granted what you do.

Rica, you designed the best book cover known to man. Okay, I might be a little biased here, but I truly cannot express how much of a pleasure it was to work with you. You brought my vision to life, and we are forever connected.

Lastly, to my mother. I love you more than words can express. We have been through some crazy things together. And although life was not easy despite it all, I am so proud to be your son. I promise to be the best son I can be for you. I thank you for always believing in me and showering me with love. But most importantly, I thank you for teaching me how to always go after what I want and always encouraging me that I CAN DO IT. You planted a seed in me that would go on to inspire countless individuals to believe in themselves. Love you, Mom.

To the remainder of my family, friends, and team, thank you for the encouragement in supporting me throughout this endeavor and inspiring me to author this book.

To you the reader, thank you for your support and for sharing your stories and experiences with me. It would mean the world to me if you leave a review of the book. Remember to ignore what they tell you; use your "unfortunate" life circumstances to your advantage, and DO NOT ever let anyone tell you, you cannot do something always tell yourself YOU CAN DO IT!

ABOUT THE AUTHOR

James Cunningham is known for his award-winning work in the financial services industry where he served thousands of successful insurance professionals and entrepreneurs. He excelled by recruiting, developing, and leading people from all walks of life on how to build profitable and solvent businesses. He retired at the young age of thirty-seven after fourteen plus years of operating one of the most successful insurance organizations in the US. He provides consultation to business leaders, athletes, and elite achievers, teaching the principles of personal development, results-driven performance, retirement planning, and mental toughness. James is recognized as one of the most influential leaders in the financial services industry. Outside of his business endeavors he specializes in speed and development training to amateur track and field athletes who have gone on to become National Champions, Junior Olympians, and All-Americans. He earned his bachelor's degree in Sports Management and Business Administration at the University of Mount Union. He was also a former NCAA football player and track and field athlete at the school. James co-owns a successful business with his wife, Marissa. They enjoy life in Indianapolis, Indiana, with their daughter.

Made in the USA
Columbia, SC
16 January 2024